Praise for *Fix the Past or Invent the Future*

"Educational leaders today face unprecedented challenges. This book offers what we need most: practical wisdom paired with bold vision. Zhao balances critique of outdated practices with forward-looking insights on AI and student-driven learning, offering school leaders a clear path to transform education in the digital age."

—**Chris Kennedy,** Superintendent of Schools, West Vancouver, British Columbia

"Yong Zhao delivers a masterful and urgent critique of our educational paradigm that is both intellectually rigorous and deeply necessary for our times. With characteristic clarity and compelling evidence, Zhao dismantles the mythology of standardized approaches to education, exposing how our reliance on effect sizes and 'evidence-based' practices masks the fundamental truth that no intervention works for all students. This book represents a paradigm-shifting work that transcends incremental reform to offer a revolutionary vision of personalized learning. This is essential reading for anyone committed to creating an educational future that truly serves all learners."

—**Jean-Claude Brizard,** president and CEO, Digital Promise

"Yong Zhao delivers another provocative wake-up call, challenging how oversimplified trends—from growth mindset to SEL to AI—are misapplied in schools, while urging bold innovation. With sharp critiques and visionary alternatives, he maps a path toward personalized, globally connected learning. This book is the timely jolt educators need to reimagine schools for the future students deserve and our planet needs."

—**Emily McCarren,** PhD, Executive Head of School, Keystone Academy Beijing

"While institutionalized educators are considering the future of schooling, Yong works with progressive schools in the here-and-now, to personalize and harness all students to create their own future."

—**Dr. Jim Watterston,** former Dean of Faculty of Education, University of Melbourne, Australia

"Inspirational reading for those seeking to transform the world of education to align with the spirit of the human being during the age of AI. As the sunshine, rain, and soil are essential for all living things in nature, so is this book for all teachers. Yong's passion is contagious."

—**Nicole L'Heureux Flynn,** middle grades virtual educator and partner teacher, Maize Virtual Preparatory School, Maize, Kansas

"With clarity and courage, Yong Zhao dismantles contemporary myths in education and shows how we can transform schools from one-size-fits-all toward truly meeting the needs of every child. A must-read for anyone serious about shaping the future of learning."

—**Pasi Sahlberg,** author of *Finnish Lessons: What Can the World Learn from Educational Change in Finland?*

"Many university academics come across one idea and then plow that furrow for the rest of their lives. But after failing to steer his family's buffalo when he was a child in rural China, Yong Zhao has not plowed another furrow ever since. Instead, in another brilliant book, Zhao takes a torch to entire fields of malnourished ideas that have become wilted and useless after years of overproduction and overuse. No idea, traditional or progressive, is spared. Evidence-based education, prescribed curriculum, standardized testing, direct instruction, growth mindsets, social and emotional learning, grit, global competence, problem-based learning and even, to a degree, AI; all of these are burned to a cinder. But this is no destructive flame-thrower of a book for its own sake. There's significant new growth here in a constructive, creative, and practical text that points the way to an educational future where learning engages and responds to what Zhao calls the jagged profiles of all individual learners with personalization, autonomy, and meaningful relationships. You will rejoice in Yong Zhao's irreverence. But you will also take heart in his vision of a better future for our schools that, in some places, already exists."

—**Andy Hargreaves,** research professor, Boston College; visiting professor, University of Ottawa; president and co-founder, ARC Education

Fix the Past
or
Invent the Future

Also by the Author

*Catching Up or Leading the Way:
American Education in the Age of Globalization*
by Yong Zhao

Teaching Students to Become Self-Determined Learners
by Michael Wehmeyer and Yong Zhao

Fix the Past or Invent the Future

Moving Beyond One-Size-Fits-All Education

Yong Zhao

Arlington, Virginia USA

2111 Wilson Boulevard, Suite 300 • Arlington, VA 22201 USA
Phone: 800-933-2723 or 703-578-9600
Website: www.ascd.org • Email: member@ascd.org
Author guidelines: www.ascd.org/write

Richard Culatta, *Chief Executive Officer;* Anthony Rebora, *Chief Content Officer;* Genny Ostertag, *Managing Director, Book Acquisitions & Editing;* Bill Varner, *Senior Acquisitions Editor;* Mary Beth Nielsen, *Director, Book Editing;* Liz Wegner, *Editor;* Catherine Gillespie, *Graphic Designer;* Circle Graphics, *Typesetter;* Christopher Logan, *Senior Production Specialist;* Shajuan Martin, *E-Publishing Specialist*

Copyright © 2026 ASCD. All rights reserved. It is illegal to reproduce copies of this work in print or electronic format (including reproductions displayed on a secure intranet or stored in a retrieval system or other electronic storage device from which copies can be made or displayed) without the prior written permission of the publisher. By purchasing only authorized electronic or print editions and not participating in or encouraging piracy of copyrighted materials, you support the rights of authors and publishers. Readers who wish to reproduce or republish excerpts of this work in print or electronic format may do so for a small fee by contacting the Copyright Clearance Center (CCC), 222 Rosewood Dr., Danvers, MA 01923, USA (phone: 978-750-8400; fax: 978-646-8600; web: www.copyright.com). To inquire about site licensing options or any other reuse, contact ASCD Permissions at www.ascd.org/permissions or permissions@ascd.org. For a list of vendors authorized to license ASCD ebooks to institutions, see www.ascd.org/epubs. Send translation inquiries to translations@ascd.org.

ASCD® is a registered trademark of Association for Supervision and Curriculum Development. All other trademarks contained in this book are the property of, and reserved by, their respective owners, and are used for editorial and informational purposes only. No such use should be construed to imply sponsorship or endorsement of the book by the respective owners.

All web links in this book are correct as of the publication date below but may have become inactive or otherwise modified since that time. If you notice a deactivated or changed link, please email books@ascd.org with the words "Link Update" in the subject line. In your message, please specify the web link, the book title, and the page number on which the link appears.

PAPERBACK ISBN: 978-1-4166-3411-9   ASCD product #125065   n12/25
PDF EBOOK ISBN: 978-1-4166-3412-6; see Books in Print for other formats.

Quantity discounts are available: email programteam@ascd.org or call 800-933-2723, ext. 5773, or 703-575-5773. For desk copies, go to www.ascd.org/deskcopy.

Library of Congress Cataloging-in-Publication Data is available for this title.
Library of Congress Control Number: 2025035397

---

35 34 33 32 31 30 29 28 27 26   1 2 3 4 5 6 7 8 9 10 11 12

Fix the Past or Invent the Future

Acknowledgments ix
Introduction 1

Part I. Fix the Past 5

   1. Why Probability Research Doesn't Help Classrooms 7
   2. Why the Growth Mindset Can Be Stubborn Stupidity 15
   3. Why SEL Doesn't Solve Students' Social and Emotional Problems in School 23
   4. Why Short-Term Wins Can Be Long-Term Losses 31
   5. Why AI Doesn't Help in the Traditional Classroom 41

Part II. Invent the Future 49

   6. The Personalization of Learning with AI 51
   7. Problem Finding and Problem Solving 59
   8. Human Interdependence and Global Competence 67
   9. The School Within a School: A New Approach to Educational Transformation 77
  10. Where to Go from Here 85

References 97
Index 105
Study Guide 109
About the Author 115

Acknowledgments

This is a book of ideas. It's a summary of my thoughts about education, which arose from my independent research and collaborative work with colleagues, from numerous conversations with wise people, and from experiments in schools across the world. I have many people to thank. I may not be able to list everyone who has had tremendous impact on me and the ideas in this book, and I hope those I don't mention will know that I am equally grateful to them. Leading scholars David Berliner, Diane Ravitch, Gene Glass, Richard Elmore, Bill McDiarmid, and Ron Beghetto are among those who have most influenced my thinking. They have shaped my perspectives on various issues in education through their publications, as well as in conversation with me. I also reaped great benefit from co-authoring articles and books with four deans and former deans of education in three different countries: Bill McDiarmid at the University of North Carolina at Chapel Hill; Rick Ginsberg at the University of Kansas; Jim Watterston at the University of Melbourne, Australia; and Zhenguo Yuan at East China Normal University. These co-authoring experiences gave me amazing insights into educational policy issues in different countries, as well as in ways to empower students to make meaningful change.

The work experience and weekly conversations with Ron Beghetto and Bill McDiarmid about a book we co-authored were tremendously enlightening when we talked and wrote about how to help students make impact. For the past five years, I have co-hosted a weekly video podcast, *Silver Lining for Learning,* with Curt Bonk, Chris Dede, Punya Mishra, and Lydia Cao. The interviews we have conducted with education innovators all over the world have given me insights into the opportunities and challenges of educational changes on a global scale. My work with Ruojun Zhong about the educational paradigm shift from an ecological perspective provided me with a fresh perspective on educational change, for which I am forever thankful.

Many education leaders have had a significant effect on my thinking by working with me in schools and education systems. These include Peter Dawkins, former vice chancellor, Victoria University, Melbourne, Australia; Sara Glover, former director of the Mitchell Institute, Victoria University; Peter Hutton, former principal of Templestowe College, Australia; Belinda Provos, principal of All Saints College, Australia; Yingchun Zhou, principal of Chongqing #8 Secondary School, China; Hao Yongnin Hao, principal of Hong Fan Middle School, China; Peter Mader, former president of the South Australian Secondary Principals' Association (SASPA); and Mary Hudson from the Association of Independent Schools, South Australia (AISSA).

I am particularly grateful for the editing work that Bill McDiarmid provided for this book. He raised great questions, which significantly improved the content.

I am also deeply indebted to my family, who have always given me the support and time I needed to work on ideas.

As usual, despite all the benefits I have received from friends and colleagues, all and any error is mine.

Introduction

For years, the pervasive story of American education was one of decline. In 1995, educational psychologists David Berliner and Bruce Biddle published a book titled *The Manufactured Crisis: Myths, Fraud, and the Attack on America's Public Schools*. It offered convincing evidence and excellent analyses to show that the educational crisis in the United States was manufactured to advance certain political and economic agendas. This book changed my thinking about data and education, but it did not convince the country. Allegations of a crisis reappear whenever news stories about standardized test scores surface.

Most recently, a drop of a few points in the 2024 National Assessment of Educational Progress (NAEP) reading scores led to headlines such as "Reading Scores Fall to New Low on NAEP" in *Education Week* (Schwartz, 2025) and "American Children's Reading Skills Reach New Lows" in *The New York Times* (Goldstein, 2025). Over the years, the release of results of international assessments, such as the Programme for International Student Assessment (PISA) and the Trends in International Mathematics and Science Study (TIMSS), has always driven media and government officials to declare that U.S. education is in crisis or in further decline.

Whether education in the United States actually is in crisis is a ceaseless debate. Always being in crisis mode might force you to take action to get out of it. But obviously, the *kind* of action matters. Actions could be working on solving problems from the past—or ditching the past and inventing the future.

Take a problem that was plaguing big cities back in 1898. Horses were commonly used to transport people and goods; in fact, New York City had more than 170,000 horses in use at the time. With a single horse producing between 10 and 15 kilograms of manure each day, manure was overwhelming big cities, such as Paris and New York. New York City alone dealt with from one to two million kilos of horse poop daily (de Durango, 2019). The first international congress on urban planning was held in New York to solve this massive problem. No solution was found, and the conference ended early.

The solution came only years later, when automobiles began to replace horses. Who would have thought at the time that automobiles would solve an environmental and a health problem, only to become an environmental and a health problem a half century later. But that's another story. The lesson here is that some unsolvable problems cannot be fixed until a new paradigm emerges.

The perception that U.S. education is experiencing a crisis has been primarily driven by the lack of improvement in test scores and international comparisons in three subjects: reading, math, and science. Test scores in reading and math have not improved significantly since the 1970s, according to NAEP (2021). International comparisons show that U.S. students have never ranked at the top since the 1960s. *A Nation at Risk* (National Commission on Excellence in Education, 1983) sounded the warning. Now, after so many years of changes, reforms, and innovations, U.S. test scores remain the same. Isn't it time to forget about trying to fix incrementally what we have inherited from the past?

This book is about inventing a new future. Today's society differs from that of 50 years ago. So does technology, and so do today's children—and so does the world. We just can't afford to be stuck in a past that no longer serves all our children.

This book has two parts. The first part (Chapters 1–5) highlights the problems of the past, whereas the second part (Chapters 6–10) focuses on creating a better future. In Chapter 1, I cite evidence that points to a fundamental problem with our current educational paradigm: a one-size-fits-all mentality. I show that any intervention, no matter how powerful, does not work for all students all the time. Because education has had a poor reputation as an elusive science (Lagemann, 2000), educational studies have been trying to become more like a hard science for a long time. Since the 1990s, randomized controlled trials and quantitative methods have been favored in educational research. Whenever possible, randomized controlled trials have been conducted and effect sizes analyzed. But, as I point out in Chapter 1, effect sizes mask the potential danger to individual students of a given intervention.

In addition, meta-analyses have become extremely popular with researchers. Academic journals favor these studies because they aggregate findings from numerous studies into "hard numbers." Policymakers and education leaders seem easily convinced by them. There are even meta-analyses of meta-analyses. However, these studies are, in many ways, "pseudoscience with real data" (Bergeron, 2017, p. 237). Averaging the averages from multiple students largely ignores the individual students in individual classrooms taught by individual teachers in individual schools located in individual communities. The findings can hardly apply to the individual students that teachers face each day.

Chapters 2 and 3 provide more examples of why a given educational intervention does not apply to all students. Popular concepts like the growth mindset may work for some students in some contexts, but if applied blindly, the approach can be foolish. Sometimes, students need to know when to quit. Another popular idea, social and emotional learning (SEL), has a similar problem. Incidentally, meta-analyses of the effects of employing both concepts in schools provide inconclusive evidence that they work for all students.

In Chapter 4, I take a slightly different angle. I focus on time and educational outcomes. Educational interventions that seem to be effective in the short term can have less-than-successful long-term consequences, hurting such desired outcomes as creativity, curiosity, and transfer.

In Chapter 5, I discuss the potential of artificial intelligence (AI) for education. Currently, AI can be useful for teachers and students, but we cannot truly realize its potential unless the paradigm shifts. Teachers and students can use AI to help them do a better job—of teaching, in the case of teachers, and of learning, in the case of students. But is what teachers are required to teach and what students are required to learn what we need today and in the future? In this chapter, I argue that the prescribed curriculum constrains the power of AI. Instead, AI should support the personalization of learning. Students should be using it to find and solve problems.

In Chapter 6, I describe an educational paradigm that reexamines personalized learning. After critiquing the traditional definition of the term, I offer a new definition that argues that true personalization has to be done *by* students instead of *for* students. This will require a relaxation of the prescribed curriculum and changes in teacher roles.

In Chapter 7, I argue that in the age of AI, the ability to come up with new questions and seek out new problems has become one of the most needed skills. But traditional schools do not teach students to do this; they focus on teaching known answers to known problems. To help students develop this future-facing skill, all teaching should encourage students to address new, genuine problems and questions, as opposed to old, prepackaged ones.

In Chapter 8, I focus on human interdependence and global competence. By truly personalizing learning, we will help students develop their own unique interests and talents and use that knowledge to find and solve problems for others and the world. Such human interdependence goes beyond classrooms and schools to become the foundation of global competence.

In Chapter 9, I show how everyone in education—students, teachers, and school leaders—can enact transformative change. I argue that government-driven changes are often about strengthening the existing paradigm and do not improve education for all. Transformative change should take place from the bottom up instead of being imposed top-down.

Chapter 10 summarizes the elements that constitute a new paradigm of education: personalization of learning, finding and solving problems, and human interdependence. I discuss potential challenges and propose a new approach: teachers as inventors, students as partners, and school leaders as enablers.

I hope this book will inspire educators, students, parents, policymakers, and education researchers to rethink education in the age of AI, reimagine the possibilities of education with AI, and take action to shift the paradigm of education.

Part I

Fix the Past

1

Why Probability Research Doesn't Help Classrooms

I have had a problem with the popular phrase *evidence-based* in education ever since I heard it about 30 years ago. It is not that I don't believe in evidence or don't support evidence-based practices or policies. Rather, I think evidence has been used as a slogan to drive certain policies, practices, programs, and methods. There are many questions we should be asking about the nature or interpretation of that evidence, but no one is asking them.

For example, what evidence are we referring to? Evidence for whom and of whom? Who collected the evidence? When and how did they collect it? Where was it collected? Who interpreted it? How does the evidence apply to other people in other situations?

We have seen too many evidence-based policies and programs fail because we did not ask these questions. For example, in the early 2000s, No Child Left Behind's (NCLB) Reading First program provided about $1 billion each year for six years to schools with high percentages of students with low reading achievement. The program's most important element was "scientifically based reading instruction." According to then–Secretary of Education Margaret Spellings, "If ever there was a program that was rooted in research and science and fact, this is it. This is the cure for cancer" (Manzo, 2008).

But the program failed to improve students' reading and was discontinued in 2009.

A common problem with evidence is overgeneralization. Whatever scientific evidence we collect or whatever theory we come up with based on the evidence is always limited to certain conditions. Although we dream of finding a method of teaching reading or math that applies to all students all the time, it is impossible. But policymakers tend to believe in the impossible; whenever a policy is decided on, it is aimed to apply to all schools, all teachers, and all students. Education businesses love to believe in the impossible and always market their products as the most effective one for all students. Even those who call themselves researchers seem to have the same tendency. Of course, school leaders and teachers also want such effective-for-all programs and methods.

This panacea thinking has been going rampant in education. It's one major reason behind the decades-long reading war, math war, and other teaching wars and why educational quality or educational outcomes have not improved much. To improve education, we must abandon the wish for panaceas and accept the fact that no educational method works for all students.

A Matter of Probability

To prove the effectiveness of an instructional method or a program, the most scientific way is to use randomized controlled trials, a method common in medical research. You randomly select a group of people to try the new medical product, and you randomly assign them to one of two groups. You give the medical product to one group and a placebo to the other. After a given period of time, you determine the difference in outcomes between the two groups.

Effect size is usually used to measure the difference. If the effect size is large, the product is considered effective. The common effect size is measured using Cohen's d, which measures the standard difference between two means. Theoretically, Cohen's d has no upper limit, but in practice, the values often fall within a certain range: 0.20 small effect size, 0.50 medium effect size, 0.80 large effect size, 1.20 very large effect size, and 2.00 huge effect size.

An effect size of 0.50 is considered large enough to be significant. In education, effect sizes are often smaller than Cohen's threshold. For example, many educational programs produce effect sizes smaller than 0.25, and it is unusual for educational interventions to have effect sizes larger than 0.80. John Hattie (2008), well known for his work on meta-analyses of educational influences in his series of books titled *Visible Learning*, suggests that an effect size of 0.40 indicates a meaningful effect on student achievement.

Since education began to adopt the scientific method in research, effect sizes have become extremely popular. Researchers have conducted studies to find significant effect sizes of various education interventions, such as instructional methods, instructional programs, or teacher training. Education businesses have also been looking for significant effect sizes to show that their products are effective. And educational policymakers are asking researchers, evaluators, and education product makers to provide effect sizes to make a case for whatever they are advocating.

What all these people do not want us to know is that effect sizes are no more than a probability exercise. Even a very large effect size does not guarantee that an intervention will work for everyone, although it may be effective for some. In medical research, a risk-benefit analysis is always conducted to understand who benefits, who might be harmed by the product, and whether the benefit is worth the risk.

Those Who Get Hurt

Effect sizes are calculated based on the difference in outcomes of the two groups. There are different ways to calculate effect size, but the main idea is to compare the means of two groups. Hopefully, the group with the substantially larger mean is the actual treatment group.

But comparisons such as these do not take into account the fate of individuals. The large mean in the treatment group can come from half of the students who scored very high, indicating good progress, but the other half of students may not have made any progress at all or may actually have experienced a decline in their learning. The intervention, in this case, would have harmed some students.

This risk-benefit situation arises in medicine all the time. Although opioid painkillers are effective for managing severe pain, they can be addictive, cause respiratory depression, and result in overdosing for some individuals. Another drug prevents blood clots but can cause severe bleeding or hemorrhagic stroke in some people. In medicine, doctors inform patients of the risks, and patients must give explicit consent when using drugs that can cause severe side effects.

In education, it's a different matter. When an intervention is found to have a certain effect size, it is deemed to be effective. In the United States, the federal government–sponsored *What Works Clearinghouse* (WWC) generally accepts 0.25 as a significant effect size (WWC, 2020). But WWC does not give any information about the potential side effects of a given intervention or about who it might harm.

This may explain, in part, why education quality has not improved for decades, despite numerous school reforms. Such reforms and changes have typically been implemented in schools in a one-size-fits-all fashion. Once again, the new intervention is applied to all students, and, once again, some students don't benefit from it or actually get hurt by it.

The Case of Visible Learning

In 2008, John Hattie published *Visible Learning: A Synthesis of Over 800 Meta-Analyses Relating to Achievement*. A *meta-analysis* is a study of many studies that address a common research question. By aggregating results, a meta-analysis aims to provide a more precise estimate of effect sizes of similar factors or interventions. For a given intervention, one study may have found an effect size of .20, another study may have found an effect size of −0.20, and a third may have found an effect size of .00. Most likely, a meta-analysis would find that the effect size of this intervention is .00.

Based on his synthesis of more than 800 meta-analyses (and later more than 1,400), Hattie created a list of programs, factors, or interventions with different effect sizes in schools. His work has been touted as providing a solid evidence-based list of what works better or worse in producing student achievement. A reporter with the British *Times Education Supplement* (Mansell, 2008) went so far as to write this about *Visible Learning*:

It is perhaps education's equivalent to the search for the Holy Grail—or the answer to life, the universe and everything. Grappled with by teachers and educationists for millennia, the perennial question goes a bit like this: if you could change one thing about the way our schooling system is run, what would it be? Now, what is believed to be the largest ever educational research study—covering more than 80 million pupils and bringing together more than 50,000 smaller studies—has come up with the answer. (paras. 1–3)

Very quickly, *Visible Learning* became a commercial professional development program for schools and teachers in about 20 countries around the globe. School leaders and teachers were led to believe that following the list of efforts ranked high in terms of effect sizes would lead to significant improvements in student achievement. However, nearly 20 years later, we have not seen such improvements in schools that implemented Hattie's approach. There has been much criticism of *Visible Learning* (Bergeron, 2017; Terhart, 2011). The fact is, none of the interventions or factors that are deemed effective based on effect sizes work equally well for all students, and those that are deemed ineffective or less effective may actually work for some students.

P-Values—and Peanuts

Probability is the essence of all educational research. No matter how high the probability is that a certain intervention will work, it won't work for every student. Besides effect size, *p*-value is commonly used in educational research. The *p* stands for *probability*, the probability of obtaining the result at least as extreme as one observed. A smaller value indicates stronger evidence against the null hypothesis, which is a statistical assumption suggesting that any observed patterns or differences in a data set are due to chance and are not the result of a meaningful effect. For example, if a study yields a *p*-value of 0.04, it means there is a 4 percent probability that the observed data would occur if the null hypothesis were true.

There is growing criticism against the use of *p*-values in research for a number of reasons. First, *p*-values are affected by sample size. You're more likely to obtain significant *p*-values with large sample sizes. That is, even if the result is practically insignificant, the *p*-value can be significant. Second, *p*-values can lead to misinterpretation. For instance, although a *p*-value indicates the probability of obtaining results at least as extreme as those observed, assuming the null hypothesis is true, it does not measure the probability that the null hypothesis is true or the size of an effect. As a result, statistically significant results can be mistakenly considered practically significant, even when the effect size is minimal. Third, to determine statistical significance, the *p*-value is often arbitrarily set at 0.05, 0.01, or 0.10. Some researchers even move the preset value based on their findings. If the achieved *p*-value is smaller or equal to the preset value, the finding is claimed to be significant. Otherwise, the finding is considered insignificant, with no consideration of the data context. This dichotomous approach could neglect nuances in the findings. Finally, some researchers, consciously or unconsciously, manipulate data or analyses to achieve a *p*-value below the preset one, which is conventionally set at 0.05.

Take the case of Brian Wansink, a former professor at Cornell University and director of the Food and Brand Lab who engaged in *p*-hacking. His research, which focused on consumer behavior and eating habits, garnered widespread attention and influenced public health policies. After investigation and retraction of several of his studies in 2018, Cornell University concluded that Wansink had committed scientific misconduct, which led to his resignation. Wansink's case underscores the importance of ethical research practices and has sparked broader discussions about the prevalence of *p*-hacking in scientific research.

However significant the *p*-value is, we must remember that it still only captures the *probability* of something happening. Moreover, depending on the nature of the sample, the probability may not even go beyond the sample itself. In education, truly randomized samples are difficult, if not impossible, to recruit, and thus truly randomized controlled trials are rarely conducted. It is also impossible to isolate the effects of a treatment from the effects of other confounding variables. The results of many educational studies are hardly replicable beyond the class or school where the study is conducted.

Teachers and school leaders may have been forced to implement interventions based on probability, with no consideration given to individual students who may not benefit from the intervention. By way of contrast, the airline industry *does* consider its individual clients. Airlines don't serve peanuts in flight anymore, simply because a few people might experience an allergic reaction. Many restaurants have followed suit, either asking you if you have any food allergies or posting cautions about foods that may cause allergic reactions. Those in education should develop such sensitivity.

Teachers Know Better

No student is "average." In any classroom, there are individual differences—and they're vast among students. Educational systems around the world have used age to organize students into grades and have developed expectations for each age group of students, but this does not account for individual differences. Even if students' cognitive, social-emotional, psychological, and physical development followed their biological age, a year has 365 days. Those born on the first day of the year are 365 days ahead of those born on the last day. The difference is huge, especially for kindergartners and early elementary students.

Of course, students' expected development does not exactly match their age. When children come to school, they come with different capabilities, interests, personalities, and perspectives. Some may be able to read at a 3rd grade level in 1st grade, whereas others can't read at all. Those advanced readers may do poorly in math, whereas others who excel in neither math nor reading may do great in science and music.

The diversity that exists in each class makes it impossible to apply one instructional approach or one educational program to all students. If we truly want to help each and every student reach their potential, we need differentiated instruction. Better yet, we need to make education "personalizable" (Zhao, 2018c, 2023)—that is, personalized to each student (Zhao, 2024).

Teachers are vital in meeting the individual needs of students. They know the students in their classes better than any educational researcher, policymaker, or education business does. They are likely to care more about each student than about probability-based theories or interventions. They need to know that no one program or method works for all students, although various methods or interventions may work for some. For the first time ever, teachers can use new technologies to help assess student learning, curate learning resources, create learning opportunities, and track the progress of each student in their classrooms.

In Sum

Evidence-based education is, of course, a wonderful idea, but we have to be careful about what the evidence is, how it's analyzed, and the conclusions we draw from it. We should consider not only the nature of evidence and how it is interpreted but also whether the evidence-based interventions work for all students. We need to be acutely aware of the possible harm that evidence-based interventions may cause to some students, even while they may be effective for others. This is especially important for policymakers and education leaders, who are often in the midst of considering the implementation of new education programs and interventions.

2

Why the Growth Mindset Can Be Stubborn Stupidity

I was born and raised in a small village in rural China's Sichuan Province in the 1960s, during the massive political turmoil called the Great Cultural Revolution. There were no schools in my village, nor was there a pathway to get out of it through education. The village was organized as a production team under Communist rule, and every peasant worked together for the team, very much like the ants in the animated film *Antz*. My best hope was to learn to become a productive farmer. But I was malnourished, small, and physically weak. I could not do many of the farming jobs, like driving a water buffalo. When a farm school opened in a nearby village and the teacher came to my house to recruit students, my father said, "Since you are so bad at farming, why don't you go to school?" I agreed. I gave up on ever becoming a successful farmer like my father and my peers.

Giving up has been a defining characteristic of my life. I have given up many opportunities to learn interesting things. I gave up learning math as soon as I could. I gave up learning to sing or dance; in fact, I never even tried. I tried sports in college to no avail, and I failed my physical education course and had to beg the teacher to "gift" me a pass so I could graduate. After I came to the United States, many accomplished educators tried to convince me that they could teach me to play music or football, in an effort to prove that people can learn anything—if they put their minds to it. But I refused. I am sure I could have become better at playing music or football, but I doubt I would have enjoyed those activities much.

I learned about the growth mindset more than a decade ago when I shared a stage with its developer, Stanford psychology professor Carol Dweck. This influential concept had been drawing much attention in schools, so I spent some time studying it.

Defining the Growth Mindset

A *growth mindset* is the belief that an individual's abilities, intelligence, and talents can be developed and improved over time through effort, learning, and perseverance. This concept contrasts with a *fixed mindset*, the belief that one's abilities and intelligence are innate, unchangeable traits (Dweck, 2000, 2006). The concept has been used in various fields to help people become successful. Hence, the title of Dweck's popular book, *Mindset: The New Psychology of Success*.

In education, the mindset idea has been translated into training programs to help students reject a fixed mindset and replace it with a growth mindset, purportedly leading to student success. Many schools and teachers have adopted the concept and have attempted to instill such a mindset in their students.

What are the results? The research findings are inconclusive at best. The two most recent meta-analytical and systematic reviews were both published in 2023, in the same issue of *Psychological Bulletin*. One study (Burnette et al., 2023), conducted by a group of scholars at North Carolina State University, included 53 independent studies from 2002, when the first mindset intervention started, to 2020. The study found an effect size of 0.14 for academic achievement and 0.32 for mental health. The 95 percent prediction intervals for the effects of mindset training ranged from −0.08 to 0.35 for academic achievement and from 0.07 to 0.57 for mental health. The authors concluded that despite the large variations in results, the effects on both academic achievement and mental health were positive, especially when the interventions were delivered to people who were expected to benefit the most.

The other study (Macnamara & Burgoyne, 2023), conducted by researchers at Case Western University, included 63 independent studies that involved more than 97,000 students. The researchers identified major shortcomings in all aspects of the studies they reviewed, including flawed study design, flawed analyses, and flawed reporting, as well as researcher and publication bias. For example, the review found that authors with financial incentives to discover positive findings reported significantly larger effects than those without financial incentives. Further, the overall effect size was 0.05, which the reviewers deemed insignificant. Additional analyses of subsets of the studies yielded even smaller effect sizes. Thirteen studies demonstrating that the intervention influenced student mindsets as intended had an average effect size of 0.04, and six studies with the highest-quality evidence had an effect size of 0.02. The authors of the meta-analysis concluded that the apparent effects of growth mindset interventions on academic achievement are probably due to poor study design, flaws in reporting, and publication bias. Given the findings of these two most recent studies, the best we can say is that teaching students to develop a growth mindset has, at best, a limited effect on student achievement and mental health.

These conclusions come with a number of caveats. First, the range of the effect sizes is quite wide, from –0.08 to 0.35, in Burnette and colleagues' meta-analysis. In other words, some studies found the mindset training had a negative impact. Because the effect size is so small, we can interpret the training as having no impact at all. The largest effect size is 0.35, which is significant but not truly impressive. Second, the Macnamara and Burgoyne meta-analysis found evidence of publication bias, which means journals are more likely to publish studies with statistically significant findings—that is, bigger effect sizes. It is thus entirely possible that studies that found smaller, negative, or zero effect sizes were not published. Third, another troubling concern is that the authors of the second review discovered that some researchers may have had financial incentives to publish results showing larger effect sizes than researchers without such incentives. This is yet another reason we should not be too confident about the findings. Overall, the alleged effects of the growth mindset are questionable.

It Just Doesn't Make Sense

There is no question that an individual's abilities, intelligence, and talents can be developed and improved over time through effort, learning, and perseverance. But the question is, *what* abilities, intelligence, and talents? No one generic ability, intelligence, or talent applies to every field, career, or job. To develop expertise in a certain field requires a significant time commitment, dedication, and deliberate practice. Malcolm Gladwell (2008) popularized the idea of the 10,000-hour rule for becoming an expert, based on research done by K. Anders Ericsson (1996). More recent research suggests the time needed is significantly higher—15,000 hours or more, depending on the skill. When time is spent developing abilities in one field, it's not available elsewhere.

More important, as Ericsson and Pool (2016) noted in *Peak: Secrets from the New Science of Expertise*, it is not only about the amount of time you spend but also about how you spend that time. Ericsson introduced the idea of *deliberate practice*, focused and goal-oriented activities designed to improve specific aspects of performance, often under the guidance of a coach or mentor. This contrasts with general practice or repetition, highlighting that not all practice leads to expertise. Of course, you are more likely to improve—and to commit more time to improving—when you engage in tasks and activities that interest you.

We humans are born with multiple or different types of intelligences. These varied intelligences reflect individuals' potentials to learn different skills or domains of knowledge (Gardner, 1983; Sternberg, 1988). Some easily learn challenging math concepts, whereas others excel at mastering foreign languages. Some may be adept at dancing or sports, whereas others have extraordinary vocal talent. However, just because you show a promising talent in one area doesn't mean you can transfer that talent to other activities. The accomplished singer may be terrible at math, and the athlete may lack an aptitude for learning foreign languages.

Further, developing abilities (or intelligence or talents) requires resources. Those whose families can afford private coaching or instruction are more likely to develop their innate ability or intelligence faster and more fully than those with fewer resources. Opportunities matter as well. Possessing a natural born talent and having the opportunity, resources, and time needed to develop it are, in many ways, a matter of randomness (Lewontin, 2001).

People also must decide where to invest their limited time and effort. For example, a student can devote time, say, to theoretical physics, for which they have little innate potential or interest, simply because teachers want them to do so. The person can persevere and study physics intently for 10,000 hours, although had they spent those 10,000 hours on something else—say, organic chemistry—for which they *do* have talent and interest, they would have had a more successful result. Similarly, a student could be encouraged to persist in studying abstract mathematics, but because they're impoverished, they lack needed resources, such as mentors or tutors.

I wasn't interested in cultivating a growth mindset in farming, math, sports, or music. This doesn't mean, however, that I did not believe I could improve my abilities, intelligence, or talents, especially in languages and programming, in which I had a strong interest. On the other hand, applying a growth mindset for a skill or knowledge domain for which one lacks talent, interest, resources, or opportunity is a waste of time. In such circumstances, relying on a growth mindset is simply stupid.

Learning to Quit

Another concept that has entered the conversation is *grit* (Duckworth, 2016). In psychology, *grit* refers to a noncognitive trait that enables individuals to maintain their determination and motivation over long durations, even in the face of failure and adversity. Popularized by psychologist and professor Angela Duckworth at the University of Pennsylvania, grit captures behavioral patterns similar to those associated with a growth mindset.

Both grit and the growth mindset emphasize the importance of resilience, persistence, and the "stick to it" spirit, and they're both useful concepts under specific circumstances. But if something persistently fails to work out, it makes sense to walk away. Unfortunately, too many people, misled by the concept of the growth mindset or grit, keep trying to improve in the same thing, even when there is little or no hope of success. They don't quit because they don't see any other way, they feel embarrassed, they worry about being ridiculed, or they do not want to waste the time and resources they have already invested. The *sunk cost fallacy* leads us to persist in doing something when rationally it makes no sense. It's like continuing to watch a boring movie because you paid $12 for a ticket or only continuing as a marketing major in college because you're halfway to a degree. To help people see the light, Annie Duke (2022), a world-class poker player, wrote *Quit: The Power of Knowing When to Walk Away*.

In education, learning to quit can be difficult because the adults that students look up to usually don't want them to quit. They genuinely believe that with effort, persistence, and resilience, students can learn, improve, and achieve. And this is not necessarily wrong. But the crucial questions are these: How much better can a student get in a given area, and what is their ceiling? If a student struggles with Algebra II but is talented and interested in writing fiction, shouldn't parents or teachers let them drop math and pursue writing?

Long-standing social expectations and norms, shared by parents, educators, and students, dictate that students should perform well in all the core school subjects—that is, in math, reading, science, and social studies. By the end of each grade, all students should have mastered certain knowledge and skills prescribed by the state. This expectation puts intense pressure on educators and parents, who then pass on the pressure to students. Perhaps, in the rapidly developing age of AI, they should be asking whether all students should be learning the same things and learning those things at the same speed. Might students quit studying what they are not good at or interested in and learn something else?

In Sum

Of course, everyone should believe that they're capable of learning, that intelligence is malleable, and that they can improve their abilities, talents, and intelligence. But we should be careful applying the concept across the board in schools. Some students may already have a strong growth mindset. Do they need more mindset training to build on their strengths? Or, instead, do they need help understanding the need to be selective in how they direct their growth mindset, or, if warranted, when it's best to quit?

Instead of expecting all students to develop a growth mindset and excel in every subject, we should allow greater flexibility. This means enabling students to focus on their strengths and interests and learn to make informed decisions about when to persist and when to quit. This approach, which we might call a *meta-growth mindset* or *gritty mindset*, could generate more productive and personalized learning experiences.

3

Why SEL Doesn't Solve Students' Social and Emotional Problems in School

Social and emotional learning (SEL) seems to be doing well. According to a report (2024) from the Collaborative for Academic, Social, and Emotional Learning (CASEL), 83 percent of school principals reported that their schools used an SEL curriculum in the 2023–24 academic year. That's up from 76 percent in 2021–22 and 46 percent in 2017–18. In addition, according to the same report, 49 states plus the District of Columbia support policies for SEL at the state level (Skoog-Hoffman et al., 2024).

At the same time, students' social and emotional states have worsened. Children's mental health issues began rising around 2012 (Haidt, 2024). Data from the Centers for Disease Control and Prevention (CDC) show that the suicide rate among Americans ages 10 to 24 rose by 62 percent between 2007 and 2021. One in three teenage girls considered taking her life in 2021, which rose from one in five in 2011 (Solomon, 2024).

If SEL programs work, shouldn't the number of students facing social and emotional challenges decline? Or does it mean that schools saw the increase in social and emotional issues among students and then decided to implement SEL programs? Will the rising rate of schools adopting SEL lead to a decline in the number of students who are feeling depressed, anxious, or meaningless?

The Rise of SEL

In 1994, CASEL was established to address the "missing piece" in education—that is, social and emotional learning. The ideas were based on the work of James Comer and colleagues at Yale University in the 1960s. They created programs to support "the whole child" in two New Haven, Connecticut, schools. Later on, in the 1980s, New Haven established the social development program to infuse SEL strategies across K–12 classrooms (CASEL, n.d.).

CASEL existed for almost 10 years before its advocacy gained footing in schools. For example, in 2011, Illinois was the only U.S. state that had adopted SEL standards, Illinois being the state that CASEL is based in. By the end of the decade, however, the number of states rose to 18. This was primarily due to the changes in U.S. federal education law. In 2015, President Obama signed into law the Every Student Succeeds Act (ESSA), which tweaked No Child Left Behind and allowed states and schools to have multiple measures of student success beyond standardized tests. Because of decades-long criticisms among educators of standardized accountability tests, many states and schools quickly picked up students' social and emotional learning as a new measure (Zhao, 2020a).

Then came the COVID-19 pandemic. Schools had to close and send students home. In a matter of weeks, schools had to organize online learning, with both teachers and students confined to their homes. The lack of outdoor activities and in-person interactions, as well as the economic and social turmoil the pandemic caused, challenged students' and teachers' psychological, social, and emotional states, forcing them to adjust to an unprecedented reality. Students' social and emotional health deteriorated globally. When students came back, schools were eager to help them return to normal—academically, socially, and emotionally. SEL had an excellent opportunity to flourish in schools.

A Lack of Evidence

The literature on SEL is voluminous, mostly praising it as what education needs to develop the whole child and help students achieve a sound social and emotional state. At the same time, critics have derided SEL, calling it a "nonacademic Common Core" (Gorman, 2016); "the latest big education fad" (Robbins, 2016); a terrifying experiment in "social and emotional engineering" (Eden, 2019); an "Orwellian idea" (Effrem & Robbins, 2019); and a hoax with roots in "faux psychology" (Finn, 2017). Much of the criticism is driven by ideology and does not have much to do with the actual effects of SEL. Although I'm not particularly interested in ideology, I do want children to be happy, as well as socially and emotionally well adjusted, so I looked for credible empirical evidence to see if SEL works.

SEL proponents rely on two meta-analyses to support the effectiveness of the approach. The first one was conducted by researchers associated with CASEL and published in 2011 (Durlak et al., 2011). The study examined the effects of 213 SEL programs that involved 270,034 students in kindergarten through high school. Based on their analysis, the authors reached a positive conclusion:

> Current findings document that SEL programs yielded significant positive effects on targeted social-emotional competencies and attitudes about self, others, and school. They also enhanced students' behavioral adjustment in the form of increased prosocial behaviors and reduced conduct and internalizing problems, and improved academic performance on achievement tests and grades. While gains in these areas were reduced in magnitude during follow-up assessments and only a small percentage of studies collected follow-up information, effects nevertheless remained statistically significant for a minimum of six months after the intervention. Collectively, these results build on positive results reported by other research teams that have conducted related reviews examining the promotion of youth development or the prevention of negative behaviors. (p. 13)

The authors seem to have good reasons for reaching such a conclusion. The average effect sizes are statistically significant, with 0.69 for SEL skills, 0.24 for attitudes, 0.28 for social behavior, 0.24 for conduct problems, 0.28 for emotional distress, and 0.28 for academic performance.

Another meta-analytical study was published in 2023 and conducted by researchers also associated with CASEL, including one of the authors from the previous meta-analysis (Cipriano et al., 2023). This study included 424 independent studies covering 252 universal school-based (USB) SEL interventions that involved 575,361 students. These are the reported effect sizes: overall, 0.194; SEL skills, 0.219; attitudes/beliefs, 0.209; prosocial behaviors, 0.178; externalizing behaviors, 0.162; creative attitudes/behaviors, 0.255; peer relationships, 0.222; emotional distress, 0.140; school functioning, 0.122; disciplinary outcomes, 0.183; school climate/safety, 0.293; family relationships, 0.061; and physical health, 0.160. Based on the findings, the authors also reached a positive conclusion: "Overall, students who participated in USB SEL interventions experienced improved academic achievement, school climate, school functioning, social emotional skills, attitudes, and prosocial and civic behaviors, and reduced internalizing and externalizing problems" (p. 15).

It is interesting to note the difference in effect sizes between the two studies, which were conducted about 10 years apart. There is an apparent drop in effect sizes from the 2011 study to the 2023 study. The 0.69 effect size can be considered large in the first study, but it refers to assessed SEL skills—that is, you teach someone these skills and then you assess them directly. It should come as no surprise that the effect size is large, but the question to ask is this: How much of the teaching translated from knowledge of the skills to actual social, emotional, and behavioral improvements?

The other effect sizes listed in both studies are moderate at best. It would be a mistake to treat this as overwhelming evidence of the effects of SEL curricula or programs. More important, both studies mentioned issues with the quality of the studies and assessment tools employed. The design of the studies could be much more improved, and there are not many good assessments of the newly added traits such as social and emotional skills. Another factor is time. Does the SEL intervention lead to long-term improvement, or is the improvement short-lived?

Of course, the biggest problem that meta-analyses' results pose is their reliance on averaging the effect sizes of individual studies.

As explained in Chapter 1, effect sizes are generalizations of the effects across a population and, consequently, do not capture the effects of the intervention on any given individual. In a school or class that implements SEL programs, some students benefit from them, some are unaffected, and some may actually be harmed. The mission of any school or class is to help each student—and not a select few—grow. Forcing the same program on all students may undermine this goal.

The Wrong Prescription

Education should be about the whole child. There is no question that schools should work hard to help every child grow socially and emotionally. But are SEL programs the right prescription for all students? In particular, are such programs right for each *individual* student? Making them a state standard or curriculum requirement pressures school leaders and teachers to find ways to implement them in their schools and classes, which requires financial resources, time in the already crowded curriculum, and professional development for teachers. The ones who certainly benefit from the state requirement are SEL commercial vendors who sell their programs to schools and provide professional development.

SEL proponents believe that five core elements are essential for personal and social development. *Self-awareness* is the recognition of one's emotions, strengths, and limitations and an understanding of how they affect behavior. *Self-management* is the effective regulation of emotions, thoughts, and behaviors, such as being able to manage stress, control impulses, and set and achieve goals. *Social awareness* is understanding and empathizing with others from diverse backgrounds and cultures, recognizing social norms, and identifying resources and supports. *Relationship skills* are about establishing and maintaining healthy and rewarding relationships through effective communication, active listening, cooperation, negotiation, and seeking or offering help when needed. *Responsible decision making* is about making ethical, constructive choices about personal and social behavior by evaluating the consequences of various actions and considering the well-being of oneself and others.

Theoretically, there is nothing wrong with these five elements. Of course, there could be other perspectives on what counts as social and emotional skills and what makes one socially and emotionally sound. For instance, some cultures might add understanding one's obligation to the larger community and the role of community health in supporting an individual's well-being.

My concern is more practical. Even if we agree with these skills, they vary depending on context and individual human beings. It is also difficult to imagine that all students develop the same set of social and emotional skills. Reducing our complex social and emotional capabilities to a set of uniformly defined skills ignores both human diversity and potentials and leads to a dull society. To become socially and emotionally mature requires time and a variety of experiences. Individuals interact with different people in different situations; encounter a range of problems; and learn from books, media, families, friends, and other sources about social and emotional capabilities. It is unlikely that an SEL curriculum or program can truly teach people to manage their emotions, interact positively with others, or make good decisions.

A More Meaningful Approach

What has caused the increase in the number of socially and emotionally challenged students? Of course, larger societal conditions are a major contributor. Political discord, challenging economic conditions, the COVID-19 pandemic, rapid changes in technology, climate change, and increasing armed conflict and warfare around the world have a great effect on our youth.

Another theory pertains to the widespread use of smartphones and social media. Young people are spending too much time on screens and often are isolating themselves from interactions with friends in the real world. They are constantly seeking "likes" from people they don't even know, and they are exposed to all sorts of "junkie" social media posts and nonsensical, possibly fake, short videos. Banning smartphones and social media in schools and limiting their use for children in general has been proposed as a solution (Haidt, 2024). Countries such as Australia and South Korea have banned smartphones in classrooms.

Perhaps a better way to think about addressing such social and emotional issues is to rethink our schools, curriculum, assessment, teaching, and student experiences, as my co-authors and I (McDiarmid et al., 2025) discussed in a recent book, *Agents of Impact: How Education Can Empower Students to Change Themselves, Their Communities, and Their World*. Why not focus on making learning more meaningful and purposeful for every student, instead of making sure we have passed on the prescribed curriculum? Why not inspire students to make their learning a self-directed, meaningful experience, which would, at the same time, reduce the smartphone distraction? Why not follow students' interests and passions to solve problems society faces so they feel empowered to improve their world?

Humanistic psychologist Abraham Maslow's hierarchy of needs is a well-known concept (Maslow, 1954, 1999). Most young people in the modern world have their basic needs met and are seeking opportunities to realize a higher level of needs. Self-actualization and self-transcendence are the highest levels; to be happy, humans need to realize their own potential to create value for others. The recently emerging positive psychology movement has provided evidence-based arguments for "authentic happiness" (Seligman, 2002). To achieve this kind of happiness, people need autonomy, accomplishment, and relationships. The sense of having self-determination, accomplishing something important, and contributing to others makes people feel good (Wehmeyer & Zhao, 2020).

To help students socially and emotionally, we don't need SEL. Instead, we need to give students the autonomy to make their own decisions about learning, the assurance that they can progress in their learning, and the ability to build relationships in and through learning. Learning should be about helping each person discover and develop their own strengths and use their strengths to serve others (McDiarmid et al., 2025). In the age of AI, the personalization of learning can help students do just that (Zhao, 2016b, 2018c, 2024).

In Sum

Education should, of course, be concerned about students' social and emotional development, in addition to their academic learning. But adding an SEL curriculum or program does not necessarily help. There's a better approach: changing schooling into meaningful and purposeful learning experiences that help each student actualize their potential and use their strengths and passions to solve problems for others.

4

Why Short-Term Wins Can Be Long-Term Losses

An interesting phenomenon has always perplexed me. Western countries, such as the United States, Australia, Canada, and the United Kingdom, have long admired education in East Asian systems, such as China, Japan, South Korea, Singapore, and Hong Kong. Numerous publications have pointed out why East Asian countries excel in education and what Western countries might learn from them. This includes a widely read and much-discussed book: *The Learning Gap: Why Our Schools Are Failing and What We Can Learn from Japanese and Chinese Education* (Stevenson & Stigler, 1992). In the 2000s, PISA found that China had the most successful education system in the world. This unleashed another wave of China envy, resulting in another wave of articles and books, such as *Surpassing Shanghai: An Agenda for American Education Built on the World's Leading Systems* (Tucker, 2011).

Ironically, at the same time, wealthy parents in East Asian countries longed to send their children to Western countries for education—and many did. Even if these children stayed in their home countries, they typically attended international schools or Western-style private schools that employ Western curricula and pedagogy and hire Western teachers who earn significantly more than local teachers. These schools are hot commodities and eagerly sought after by wealthy residents.

Conversely, I don't know of parents in Australia, the United Kingdom, the United States, or Canada who send their children to these Asian countries for their education. Nevertheless, policymakers in these countries often push for more stringent curricula, more school time, more standardized tests, more homework, and more stress, elements that characterize these high-performing East Asian school systems. Some U.S. and U.K. schools have imported "Singapore math" and math textbooks from Shanghai. Some schools in the United Kingdom have invited Shanghai teachers to come and teach in their classrooms. Academics and educational policymakers have urged U.S. teachers to prepare their lessons in a practice called "lesson study," a popular teaching method in both China and Japan (Cheung & Wong, 2014).

Although some Western policymakers and critics admire East Asian education for its superior results on international tests, East Asian countries have been looking to Western countries, particularly to the United States, to learn how to promote more creativity among their graduates (Zhao, 2018d). But little evidence exists that Western schools are educating students to be creative.

I have had the great fortune to be born in China, to have attended school there, and to have taught there for seven years before I came to the United States. During my more than 30 years in the United States, I have had plenty of experience interacting with teachers, school leaders, and educational policymakers around the globe. So I have a good sense of education in both the East and the West, and the apparent contradictions in perspectives about education led me to investigate.

The first publication that helped me think about this issue was written by Tom Loveless of the Brookings Institution in 2006. In a report comparing U.S. students with students in other education systems based on results from the Trends in International Mathematics and Science Study (TIMSS), Loveless presented the correlations between test scores and students' levels of confidence and enjoyment. He discovered a significant negative correlation in both 4th and 8th grade. Students in education systems that produced high TIMSS scores were less confident in the subjects and enjoyed school less. U.S. students' test scores were much lower than those of their counterparts in East Asia, but they seemed to have more confidence and enjoyed their experiences with the subjects more.

Many U.S. researchers think U.S. students' low test scores or achievement in math and science are due to the fact that their math and science courses are overly relaxed and not demanding and challenging enough; as a result, the students have high confidence and enjoy the courses. East Asian students, in contrast, have more challenging and demanding courses, leading to higher achievement. This is much the same argument about the difference in education between the Soviet Union and the United States in the 1950s. A *Life* magazine feature reported that students in the Soviet Union tackled tough courses and played challenging games, such as chess, while U.S. high schoolers were just having too much fun in school (Wilson, 1958).

I have a different interpretation. I thought the TIMSS results show precisely the power of U.S. education. Confidence and enjoyment are much more important in life than test scores. When people have confidence and enjoy something, they are able to learn and do interesting things in life. What helped the United States stay strong for so many decades is creativity and the entrepreneurial spirit, which require confidence and enjoyment. This led me to dig deeper to learn more.

East Versus West: What Matters in Education?

I found that U.S. students have a long history of poor performance in comparison to students in other countries. For example, in the 1960s, in the First International Mathematics Study, U.S. 12th graders ranked 12th out of 12 countries. In the First International Science Study, they ranked 14th out of 18 countries. Later on, in the second and third math and science studies, which became TIMSS, they didn't do any better, remaining pretty much the same from the 1970s to the 2000s (Zhao, 2018e). Because the PISA started around 2000, U.S. students have never performed particularly well. Among students from 70 or so education systems, U.S. 15-year-olds typically ranked in the middle.

If test scores are a reliable measure of education quality, the United States has never had a good educational system. And if education mattered in economic development, as some academics and policymakers assume, the United States should not be nearly as strong as we are today, given our mediocre test scores. Perhaps there are better indicators of education quality.

I began to look for other measurements—namely, noncognitive factors, such as confidence and enjoyment. In the 2011 TIMSS, U.S. students' average math score was 509 and British students averaged 507; both were 100 points less than Korea (613), Singapore (611), and Taiwan (609). But 24 percent of U.S. students reported they were confident in math, and 51 percent said they value math. Sixteen percent of British students reported they were confident in math, and 48 percent said they valued math. In comparison, only 3 percent of Korean students were confident and 14 percent valued math, 14 percent of students in Singapore were confident and 43 percent valued math, and 7 percent of students in Taiwan were confident and 13 percent valued math (Mullis et al., 2012). These numbers are similar to what Loveless found earlier.

I then analyzed the PISA data, as well as data from an international study of entrepreneurship, and found that PISA results in math, reading, and science all had negative correlations with entrepreneurship confidence across different countries (Zhao, 2012). In other words, education systems that produce high PISA scores have lower entrepreneurship confidence—that is, the belief that one can start and run a business. On the 2009 PISA, Singapore, Korea, Taiwan, and Japan all had high scores, easily ranking in the top 10 in the world, but their perceived entrepreneurship capability was at the bottom. In contrast, U.S. students' PISA scores were low, but they had quite high entrepreneurial confidence.

Other researchers have found that high test scores in international studies hardly predict economic or life success. For instance, Keith Baker (2007), a former U.S. Department of Education officer, found that international test scores are negatively correlated with economic development, productivity, happiness, and creativity. Education consultant Chris Tienken (2008) reported similar findings. In contrast, Eric Hanushek and Ludger Woessmann (2010, 2012) made the amazing observation that international test scores are, in fact, highly correlated with national economic growth. Their analysis had several problems, but the primary issue is that they manufactured data that did not exist, as I pointed out in an article about PISA, "Two Decades of Havoc: A Synthesis of Criticism Against PISA" (Zhao, 2020b).

We are not sure at this point that test scores do not matter, but it seems they don't matter as much as we have believed. Noncognitive factors matter, too. By the way, PISA results show a negative correlation between PISA scores and student well-being (Organisation for Economic Co-operation and Development [OECD], 2019a, 2019b). If confidence, enjoyment, valuing the subject, and social and emotional well-being are important education outcomes, how is it that high-performing education systems fail to support them?

The answer has a lot to do with the side effects of schooling (Zhao, 2017, 2018e; Zhao & Beghetto, 2024). Take school time. The 2018 PISA shows significant variations in time spent on schooling (OECD, 2019b). For example, 15-year-old students in the United States spend about 27 hours each week in school lessons, compared to 32 hours in China, 33 hours in Japan, and 35 hours in Singapore. Time spent on homework also varies, ranging from 3 hours each week in Finland to 13.8 hours in China. Moreover, the number of school days per calendar year differs globally: 180 days in the United States, 200 days in China, and up to 220 days in South Korea. Students in East Asia often devote weekends and holidays to academic studies, known as "shadow education."

Perhaps spending more time in school helps students do better in mastering academic subjects and scoring high on tests, but it takes time away from self-directed activities that could promote relaxation, greater self-efficacy, socialization, interaction with the real world, or exploration of extracurricular interests. Pedagogy matters, too. If teaching is only focused on ensuring student mastery of the content and excellent test-taking skills, the short-term effects can be stellar test scores. But the longer-term goals, such as developing confidence, social and emotional well-being, creativity, and curiosity, may suffer.

Short Term Versus Long Term: Knowledge Acquisition and Life Quality

Elizabeth Bonawitz, a psychology professor at the University of California at Berkeley, conducted an experiment with 85 preschoolers ages 48 to 72 months old in which the children were asked to play with a novel toy (Bonawitz et al., 2011). The preschoolers were randomly assigned into four conditions: one pedagogical and three non-pedagogical, which included interrupted, baseline, and naïve conditions.

In the pedagogical condition, the experimenter showed and explained to the children how to play with the toy. In the interrupted non-pedagogical condition, the experimenter did exactly the same as in the pedagogical condition, but she moved away from the scene immediately after the demonstration. In the naïve condition, the experimenter showed that the toy was new to her because she just found it, and she wanted to figure out how to play with it. In the baseline condition, the experimenter did not demonstrate how to play with the toy. Instead, she simply called the children's attention to it. In all conditions, the experimenter encouraged the children to figure out how the toy worked and then left them to play with it. The researchers recorded all sessions on video and compared the children's total amount of playing time, the number of unique actions performed, the proportion of time spent on the demonstrated function, and the total number of functions discovered.

The researchers found that "teaching constrains children's exploration and discovery. Children who were taught a function of a toy performed fewer kinds of actions of the toy and discovered fewer of its functions than children who did not receive a pedagogical demonstration" (Bonawitz et al., 2011, p. 325). If measuring whether the children had mastered the skills to play with the toy, based on the match between the children's play and the demonstrated play, those in the pedagogical condition would have done better. But is that immediate gain worth the possible loss of curiosity and creativity?

There has long been a war between inquiry-based learning and direct instruction. Direct instruction proponents have argued for its effectiveness (National Institute for Direct Instruction, 2014), but the results are often short term, the immediate outcomes of the instructed materials. The long-term side effects of direct instruction have rarely been studied, although it was pointed out in the 1970s that direct instruction may constrain the development of creativity (Peterson, 1979).

Inquiry-based learning, on the other hand, has been criticized for a lack of immediate outcomes, which ignores longer-term benefits.

An article published in 1986 compared the long-term results of direct instruction and inquiry-based education (Schweinhart et al., 1986). The study started in 1967, and the researchers compared three early childhood programs: One used a child-centered discovery learning approach, one used direct instruction, and one used a traditional (whatever that was) approach.

The study found that through age 10, the only noticeable difference among the three groups was that at age 5, children in the direct instruction group had a significantly higher average IQ score than those in the traditional nursery program. But a shocking difference was observed when the researchers expanded the measurement of outcomes to include community behavior through the age of 15. They found that the direct instruction group had reported committing two and half times more acts of misconduct than the child-centered group. In addition, children from the direct instruction group reported that they were not as well thought of by their families as the other two groups.

When the children were about 23 years old in the 1990s, a follow-up study (Schweinhart & Weikart, 1997) found that the child-centered group did better than the direct instruction group in life quality outcomes, such as highest year of schooling planned, higher percentage living with a spouse, fewer sources of irritation, fewer self-reported misconducts, fewer felony arrests, and fewer arrests for property crimes. They also had fewer years of identified emotional impairment or disturbance and were involved in more volunteer work than the direct instruction group.

Unproductive Success Versus Productive Failure: Knowledge Retention and Transfer

Even just for mastering the expected content, we need to consider short-term wins as opposed to long-term losses. Educators want students to learn fast. Teachers want to effectively teach—and, clearly, school leaders want their teachers to effectively teach—so students master what is taught. School leaders want to see high overall student achievement in the yearly standardized tests. Policymakers and educational researchers alike want students to demonstrate their learning annually in such mandated tests. In the same vein, innovative education programs want to demonstrate, using immediate test results, that their students achieve as well as, if not better than, students using traditional approaches. There have also been many debates about which approach delivers better immediate results. The reading wars and math wars are good examples of short-term gains versus long-term outcomes (Zhao, 2018e).

But short-term wins can come at the cost of long-term outcomes. Some instructional methods may deliver immediate results, but students quickly forget what they've learned after the test, whereas other methods may not appear as effective in the short term yet produce longer-lasting, deeper understanding. Manu Kapur, a professor of learning sciences and higher education at ETH, a public university in Zurich, Switzerland, used the term "unproductive success" to characterize methods that produce immediate success but do not lead to real learning in the long term. According to Kapur (2016), "it is possible for students to show high performance on memory tasks or carrying out problem-solving procedures without a commensurable understanding of what it is that they are doing" (p. 290). Kapur found that students in a direct instruction condition were initially more successful in solving well-structured problems, but in the end, their performance on tasks that required deeper conceptual understanding was inferior to that of students in the opposite condition, who had engaged in what he called "productive failure" (Kapur & Bielaczyc, 2012).

Another study showed similar effects. Conducted by David Klahr, a Carnegie Mellon University psychologist, and Milena Nigam, director of applied research and evaluation at the University of Pittsburgh, the study found that direct instruction was much more effective in teaching 3rd and 4th graders a science concept than the child-centered inquiry-based approach. Moreover, the children in both groups were equally good at applying the concept to authentic contexts the following day. The researchers concluded that direct instruction can produce more successful learning without sacrificing the longer-term goal of transfer (Klahr & Nigam, 2004). But their conclusion was proven wrong by two psychologists at Teachers College, Columbia

University: David Dean, Jr. and Deanna Kuhn. These two researchers conducted a study almost identical to that of Klahr and Nigam and found that although direct instruction "is capable of producing a significant level of correct performance . . . immediately following instruction," at week 11 after the instruction, the performance of students in the direct instruction group began to disappear (Dean & Kuhn, 2007, p. 394). By week 17, it had fallen much lower.

In Sum

In high-stakes accountability systems that use standardized test scores, students, teachers, school leaders, policymakers, and the public tend to focus on immediate outcomes. This chapter brings evidence to show that immediate positive outcomes can have long-term negative effects. The high scores of students in East Asia come at the cost of students' confidence and opportunities to explore their interests and the world at large. Direct instruction's immediate success comes at the cost of creativity, long-term transfer, and student well-being. In contrast, some education programs and methods that do not seem to produce immediate acquisition of knowledge have long-term benefits and support the development of the whole child. This is so very important today, when we are preparing students for a quickly changing, uncertain world. Because there are more important things than knowledge acquisition and test taking, we need to think about teaching and learning in a different way.

5

Why AI Doesn't Help in the Traditional Classroom

Within two months of its release in November 2022, ChatGPT gained more than 100 million users, making it the fastest-growing consumer software application in human history (Hu, 2023). Many other similar platforms emerged. It is very likely that the total number of generative AI platform users could easily reach into the billions in 2025.

I was among the first to use ChatGPT and other emerging AI tools, such as Google's Gemini and Anthropic's Claude. I've used AI for research, brainstorming ideas, getting feedback and suggestions on my writing, and summarizing major points of articles or conversations. Two colleagues (Bill McDiarmid and Ron Beghetto) and I wrote a book in close collaboration with ChatGPT and other AI tools (McDiarmid et al., 2025). We treated AI as a co-author, and it provided a lot of help. For example, AI found and added references to our drafts and analyzed our weekly online conversations.

I have started teaching a graduate course at the University of Kansas about AI and its use in educational research. I have also been deeply involved in efforts to use AI to personalize the learning of K–12 students. I have used AI to develop problem-based creativity and entrepreneurship education curriculum and learning materials for high school students. I have worked with schools and teachers on how to use AI in education. And I have discussed AI with many educational researchers, read many publications, and attended many presentations on this topic.

One of the most important things I have learned over these past two years is that AI has great power—and it will create problems in the traditional classroom.

Training on AI: It's Easier Than You Think

Educators have faced tremendous pressure because of generative AI, as have educational system leaders and policymakers. Should students be allowed to use tools such as ChatGPT in school? How can teachers incorporate AI in their teaching, and how can school leaders help? What can we do to ensure that students do not use AI to cheat in their homework and exams?

Since the release of ChatGPT, workshops, conferences, research publications, online courses, and all sorts of professional development programs about AI and its use in education have mushroomed. Schools and teachers can easily find an expert to talk to about how they can use AI. But educators can get the same information directly from AI. For example, a teacher can ask ChatGPT, "How can I use AI to teach my 4th grade math class?" AI will quickly provide a list of strategies and suggestions for resources. It will also likely include tips for personalized learning; tools to use for lesson planning and generating materials; and resources to help teachers with interactive problem solving, differentiated instruction, and even grading student work.

Teachers can explore the suggested tools and resources and then ask ChatGPT to be more specific about each lesson or each mathematical concept. They can also describe the conditions of the classroom or of specific students and get specific answers. They can use AI tools for personalized professional development to become completely competent in using AI without the help of so-called AI experts.

What teachers need is the belief that they can actually do this. Generative AI tools, such as ChatGPT, are natural language systems; they were made to communicate with ordinary people using natural language instead of computer code. AI tools have amassed a huge collection of human knowledge and provide easy ways to access it.

Teachers can start using AI in their teaching right now; the more they use it, the more competent they will become.

Teachers also need time to explore AI. They're already overworked, and their time is precious. But the fact is, after a small initial investment of time, AI can drastically improve teacher efficiency.

Cheating is one of the biggest concerns of teachers when it comes to AI. Today, generative AI tools can outperform the average human being on any kind of exam or homework. Although many schools have banned the use of AI, it is impossible to prevent students from using it. There is not much that teachers can do—unless they develop new work for students that deliberately assumes that students will use, or that requires them to use, AI.

No Possibility to Transform

First of all, although teachers can use AI to improve their teaching, the power of AI is hardly needed in the traditional classroom, just as traditional teaching didn't need other modern technology (Ginsberg & Zhao, 2023). Teachers have certainly used such tools as smartboards, PowerPoint, and search engines, and they may have looked to AI to create lesson plans, teaching materials, homework, and even tutoring help for some students. But these tools have not transformed teaching; conventional teaching has remained the same as it was 50 years ago.

Second, the prescribed curriculum and associated pedagogical methods have been established for a long time. Materials for teachers and students have been well developed and are easily accessible. New materials are not needed. Interested teachers could use AI to prepare lessons, grade homework and exams, write comments to students, or reply to emails, but these uses do not take advantage of the transformative power of AI.

Third, the traditional way that classes are organized and taught prevents AI from transforming student learning. In the traditional class, teachers dominate with lectures and teacher-organized learning activities. Little time is available for students to exercise their autonomy. Moreover, what each class is supposed to teach is predefined. All students are supposed to learn the same thing, complete the same work, and pass the same exams. The only option students have for using AI is to help with learning the content and doing the homework.

There is a joke about AI in the traditional classroom that captures the essence of this. Teachers use AI to create teaching plans and develop student work. Students use AI to do the work. Then teachers use AI to grade student work. Essentially, AI has done everything in teaching and learning.

The Real Power of AI

Generative AI changes rapidly. It is difficult to imagine what it might be able to do in a year or two. But from an education perspective, we do not need to speculate about how it will evolve. Instead, we need to think of how it could affect education.

Redefining Society and the Economy

AI, not only generative AI, has already redefined the knowledge and abilities that will be more or less useful. It will continue to do so by rapidly disrupting the existing economic and social orders. Routine and mechanical jobs will continue to be replaced by machines. A report by the Brookings Institution (Muro et al., 2019) that appeared a few years before the arrival of ChatGPT paints an accurate picture of other jobs that AI will disrupt: high-paying ones and those requiring degrees. Today, AI has already replaced numerous jobs in accounting, basic coding, text editing, legal affairs, design, and even medicine. It has already been used to advance scientific research, speed up drug development, draft stories and movie scripts, and assist in engineering and artistic design. It is difficult to imagine a field that has not been affected by AI.

Although it devalues some human skills, AI increases the value of others. Creativity and the entrepreneurial spirit have become more important. AI may provide excellent solutions to problems, but we need creative and entrepreneurial individuals to identify and evaluate the significance of problems.

Similarly, AI has made it possible for anyone with special and unique capabilities to market their talents and expertise globally. Farmers in remote areas can directly market their products to customers anywhere in the world. Although we may poke fun at some of the online videos or online personalities, we cannot underestimate the great social, political, and economic influence they wield.

As a result, as some jobs disappear, new ones will emerge. New jobs require new capabilities and talents. For example, the traditional school curriculum has never included preparing students as online influencers, but such skills have become important. Schools traditionally have offered courses or extracurricular activities in sports, music, acting, or broadcasting, but these have been regarded as less important than reading, math, and science. However, today, abilities in such activities are valued as much as, if not more than, traditional academic skills.

AI and other technologies will undoubtedly continue to redefine human society and the economy, eroding the value of human talents, knowledge, and skills. At the beginning of the Industrial Revolution, there was much discussion about what knowledge was important. In his well-known essay *What Knowledge Is of Most Worth?*, the British philosopher Herbert Spencer (1911) argued that education should move away from the classics toward science because science was becoming much more important than Latin and Greek in society.

Today, we are faced with another revolution. Should we not reconsider to what extent our prescribed curriculum teaches valuable skills and knowledge to our children? Should we not reconsider what knowledge is of most worth today and how that has changed over the past 100 years?

The Unexpected Impact of AI on Education

"Learning has escaped the classroom," the late Harvard University education professor Richard Elmore told me several years ago. Schools still control credentialing but not learning itself. Indeed, even before the arrival of generative AI, plenty of learning resources, including video, audio, text, and multimedia materials, were available online

(Zhao, 2022b). As I have joked about, American Thanksgiving dinner certainly tastes better than 20 years ago because we have more recipes to follow than just that one from Grandma.

Today, with the addition of generative AI, students can literally learn anything. I have recently been learning sciences from ChatGPT. When I was young, I did not have access to good science courses, and my teachers barely understood what they were teaching in my rural schools. So, for example, I didn't learn the basics of electricity. When I asked ChatGPT to explain these concepts, it produced easy-to-understand explanations and materials. I can ask it to present the information in Chinese, my native language, or in English. I can also ask it to present it in different ways using different analogies, in audio or in text. And I can do this anytime in any place. I couldn't get a more patient teacher.

Of course, I am not suggesting that schools are no longer useful. K–12 students are learning much more than just content. They need to develop social skills, character, and a host of other noncognitive capabilities that are best learned in groups. But new options have begun to appear. For example, we have seen a growth of virtual public schools for K–12 students in the United States. During the 2019–20 school year, before the COVID-19 pandemic, nearly 300,000 students enrolled in virtual schools (National Center for Education Statistics, n.d.). Virtual schools have likely become even more popular post-COVID. There are also those parents who homeschool their children and who seek help from virtual schools, online tutoring, and online resources. In fact, homeschooling may improve significantly because of the resources and tools now available to both parents and students.

Nevertheless, the percentage of students enrolled in online schools is still small, and most online schools still teach students in a traditional way. Many students enroll in online schools simply to fulfill state requirements for graduating high school. But what if virtual schools offered something different?

Because of technology, today's young people can participate in the real economy. They can produce their own music, videos, or online programs. And they're not just performers. They are computer programmers, text editors, fiction and nonfiction writers, image and video editors, and science and engineering researchers. Just as the legal system must evolve to accommodate the increasing diversity of jobs that young people can do in the modern world (Friedman, 2022), so, too, must education.

Young people are now able to do authentic jobs. Should schools prevent them from doing so? Or should schools simply be satisfied by engaging students in project-based learning, an approach that usually does not lead to creating authentic products or solving real problems? Perhaps schools should consider teaching students to take on real jobs—ones that are appropriate for their age—and learn through doing those jobs.

In Sum

AI is powerful and is leading a revolution in human social, political, and economic life. It has tremendous value for education, but its potential cannot be realized in the traditional schooling arrangement with the same old curriculum, classroom, pedagogy, and assessment (Zhao, 2025). Unless schools change, problems such as cheating are likely to worsen. Teachers don't need special training in AI. They can learn how to use it themselves.

The true power of AI lies in its great potential to redefine human talents (Zhao et al., 2022). Because of the disruptions it's causing in industry, AI will likely make some knowledge and skills less valuable and others more valuable. AI poses significant challenges to schooling because students can learn any content now using this multidisciplinary, multimodal, and generative tool. Instead of thinking about AI within the traditional framework of schooling, schools need to rethink the prescribed curriculum, prescribed learning pathways, and prescribed classroom-based learning. Do we still need them? Is it time to end the traditional "grammar of schooling" (Zhao, 2024)?

Part II

Invent the Future

6

The Personalization of Learning with AI

If I ask AI, "How can we use AI in education?" here is its number one reply: for personalized learning. Of course, AI doesn't consciously "think" or "predict" this response. Rather, the response appears in the huge amount of existing data that has been used to train AI.

Because it emerges from the existing literature, the type of personalized learning that AI recommends is decidedly Skinnerian (Watters, 2023). B. F. Skinner, one of the most influential behaviorist psychologists, developed a teaching machine in the 1950s. This mechanical device presented educational content in a structured manner. It typically displayed a problem or question through a small window, and students would write their responses. The machine then provided immediate feedback, reinforcing correct answers and guiding students through positive reinforcement. The device enabled students to progress at their own pace (Skinner, 1968).

In essence, Skinner invented the machine for personalized learning. Today, numerous computer- and AI-assisted personalized systems have similar features: They present a question or problem, provide feedback on student responses, and present needed information or instruction to correct that response, thus enabling students to progress at their own pace. Skinner had great hopes for his invention and predicted an education revolution. As he wrote,

> The task can be stated in concrete terms. The necessary techniques are known. The equipment can easily be provided. Nothing stands in the way except cultural inertia.... We are on the threshold of an exciting and revolutionary period in which the scientific study of man will be put to work in man's best interests. Education must play its part. It must accept the fact that sweeping revision of educational practice is possible and inevitable. (1954, p. 86)

The revolution did not happen. Over the past 70-some years, several technologies have provided various forms of personalized learning. We've had computer-assisted instruction, then online personalized learning, and today AI-driven personalized learning. But we are still waiting for the revolution in education that Skinner promised.

The Problem with a Prescribed Curriculum

The real problem lies with our education paradigm, which assumes that all students should learn the curriculum at the same pace, follow the same pedagogy, and pass the same exam. It also assumes that all students have the same interests; the same capability; and the same community, family, and school conditions. It further assumes that all students graduating with this same repertoire of skills and knowledge will find gainful employment and have a happy life.

Students could be allowed to learn at their own pace, but they still must pass the same exams or demonstrate they have mastered the same content. They can also learn in different places and at different times, but ultimately what they learn and how they are assessed are the same as what everyone else is learning and being assessed on because of the prescribed accountability requirements of the state in which they live.

This paradigm is deeply flawed. We know students differ on multiple dimensions. They aren't interested in the same school subjects, nor do they have similar aptitudes for the various disciplines. They come from different families and communities. They do not learn or develop in the same way or on the same schedule. They ultimately will work at jobs that require different knowledge and skills. Finally, this model has never provided equal educational opportunities for all.

Various innovative approaches to improve this paradigm have failed. So have the numerous reform efforts that tried to make this paradigm more equitable and effective. The problem with reforms is that they've tried to change everything except the prescribed curriculum. In fact, the reforms are typically intended to *reinforce* the prescribed curriculum through standardized testing and improved pedagogy (Zhao & Zhong, 2024; Zhong & Zhao, 2025). Educational innovations, including personalized learning, have been co-opted to do the same.

Student Autonomy: A Focus on Interests and Strengths

In the history of education, innovations and reforms have touched every aspect of schooling, from curriculum to pedagogy, from assessments to learning methods, and from student grouping to the organization of teaching. What they *haven't* touched is the prescribed curriculum. There seems to be a general consensus that all students should learn the same content. State authorities mandate the curriculum and reinforce it with assessments. Even private schools offer a common curriculum. Colleges further reinforce the prescribed curriculum by requiring the inclusion of student grades in admissions applications. Parents also know what their children are expected to learn—which is typically what *they* were expected to learn as students. Teachers are trained to teach this curriculum, and students are expected to learn it. As a result, the prescribed curriculum dominates students' school life. Little time is allocated for students to follow their interests.

As I've noted previously in this book,

- No one can guarantee that the prescribed curriculum teaches all students what they need to thrive in the uncertain age of AI. Schools should therefore allow students some autonomy over what they learn.
- Schools serve a wide variety of students, and the prescribed curriculum does not meet each individual student's needs. We

need to diversify course offerings so that students have more autonomy over the subjects they choose to study.
- Students develop differently, and no one education intervention works for all. The prescribed curriculum should have space for students to learn and master the required content at their own pace.
- In the age of AI, students can follow their interests using AI tools. Allowing student autonomy in learning with and through AI helps them develop AI literacy, as well as the ability to co-evolve with AI.
- Learning to manage their own learning is essential for students to become lifelong learners. Being able to responsibly manage their autonomy and self-determination and use these skills to solve meaningful problems helps students become more socially and emotionally engaged with schools and life.

If schools and education systems are willing to relax the prescribed curriculum and give students more autonomy, we can imagine a different kind of personalized learning. With support from teachers and parents, students should be able to explore and decide what they want to learn, how they want to learn it, and how they can assess their learning.

Indeed, students need to know fundamental information and concepts that are shared in common with others to perform their duties as citizens of a society and members of a community and to participate in public discourse. The percentage of the curriculum that students might design would vary depending on the society and school (Zhao, 2022b).

Schools need to determine how much time to afford students during the school day to personalize their learning. A school might start with a one-hour course called "personalized learning" that students could take five days a week. In this course, students would explore their interests and decide what they want to learn and how they want to learn it in collaboration with teachers and their classmates. Gradually, the school could give more time for personalized learning and less time for the prescribed curriculum.

Schools should also consider changing student age as the basis for determining the sequence of content in a curriculum. To start, education systems and schools should focus on engaging students instead of narrowly channeling student access to learning opportunities. For instance, many U.S. states have passed laws holding back 3rd graders who do not pass the state reading test. A systemic review of data shows that reasons for retention are more political than scientific, without significant benefits to students (Hauser, 2000). Schools have also been requiring students to attend remedial reading and math programs, which take time away from attending more engaging and meaningful school activities. Perhaps a better approach is to personalize a path to mastering the basic requirements in the prescribed curriculum. This might mean allowing some students more time to meet state expectations.

Students may not know how to personalize their learning in the beginning. In fact, in traditional schools, students have not been allowed to think they *could* develop their own courses. And in some cases, students may never have thought that their interests even matter. As a result, some students may only know that they're not very interested in some school subjects or activities, but they do not exactly know what they are interested in. Teachers could help students discover and cultivate their interests by exposing them to more possibilities; by doing so, student interests would most likely evolve.

Student strengths, rather than their weaknesses, could be the starting place. All students have a jagged profile of talents, abilities, knowledge, skills, and personalities (Rose, 2016). Personalization helps students identify their strengths instead of trying to fix their deficits (Zhao, 2016b). The idea is to focus on what students *can* do and encourage them to do more of it so that they have a sense of progress, confidence, and accomplishment.

Because schools don't typically create opportunities for students to discover their strengths, students may not be aware of them. By engaging in a variety of projects and activities, students would have a greater opportunity to discover both their strengths and weaknesses. If they find that they lack either the ability or interest in some field, they can move on to explore different ones.

Personalized learning starts with giving students autonomy to self-determine their own learning process. The key is not to force students into learning something they have no interest or strength in. An unintended consequence, for instance, of pushing students to study calculus when they lack the interest or ability can result in them hating and avoiding all math. Also, enabling students to explore possibilities outside the traditional prescribed curriculum helps them develop a broader perspective of the real world, as well as the understanding that they can actually do something to make that world a better place (McDiarmid et al., 2025).

A New Role for Teachers and Schools

Personalization of learning requires more changes than just changing the prescribed curriculum (Zhao & Zhong, 2024; Zhong & Zhao, 2025). To support personalized learning, teachers need to focus on the process through which students discover and develop their interests and strengths. They are no longer primarily the content experts because students will turn to AI and other technological tools for that content.

Teachers acquire the role of *process facilitator* in personalized learning (Zhao, 2018a, 2022a). This requires them to respond to the particular situation a student finds themself in. For example, teachers may need to be the guide for students who are confused and looking for direction. Sometimes, they may need to be the emotional support person when students meet with defeat or do not feel motivated. Sometimes, they may need to be the project manager when students are not making as much progress as they should. Sometimes, they may need to be the resource curator when students cannot find the information they're looking for from AI and technology. Sometimes, they may need to be the communicator with parents, students, and the public. Teachers in this scenario are more like personal coaches who understand their students and can connect them to a broader world, provide resources, and deliver feedback.

In other words, teaching itself is *personalizable*. Teachers are undoubtedly necessary in schools, but they do not need to drive the learning. Instead, they can be led by students. Each student may have different needs at different times, and teachers should respond to individual needs with individual responses.

Traditional teacher education has not focused on preparing teachers to support personalized learning, and the majority of teachers have not had experience with personalizable teaching. Many teachers might find this task unfamiliar and challenging. However, if they are willing to accept the idea that students can learn content and develop skills on their own without being explicitly taught, and if they can abandon the idea that they must teach content, teachers can work with students to develop necessary new skills. As the Chinese saying goes, "Teaching and learning promote each other."

First, teachers can stop lecturing to all students and begin responding to individual students' needs. Second, teachers can work on organizing materials for different students in response to individual students' needs. And finally, teachers can check on the progress of individual students and design different learning expectations for individuals.

I coined the phrase "personalizable education" in my book *Reach for Greatness: Personalizable Education for All Children* (Zhao, 2018c). Besides teaching, other aspects of schooling also can be personalized. For example, personalized learning requires access to AI and online resources, so schools need to provide internet-connected devices or, at least, not ban the use of smart devices in schools. Although there are practical and serious issues with the use of smartphones in class, we should not throw the baby out with the bathwater. Technological tools have become a necessity for learning, and they must be readily available so that students can access them whenever they need to.

School facilities and space should be personalizable as well. Students may need to use those spaces in different ways. Some newer schools have created more innovative spaces by using more flexible furniture in the classroom. Some schools have created options that enable students to learn beyond their classrooms.

There are schools that have done this to some degree. Summerhill School in England, Sudbury School in Massachusetts, and some other democratic schools allow students to have a say in their learning

(Zhao, 2012, 2016c). In Australia, Templestowe College has a personalized learning track that enables students to decide what they want to learn (Zhao, 2018c).

In Sum

Personalized learning is the way forward for educational excellence and equity. This is especially true in the age of AI. But personalized learning is not a simple process of using technology to support students as they learn the same content and pass the same test using different learning methods or pacing. Rather, personalization of learning enables students to follow their passions and develop their strengths so that they can become unique and great in their own ways. In other words, students should have the autonomy to decide what, how, and when to learn. This requires schools and teachers to reconsider the prescribed curriculum and find time and resources to do so. Personalization should be done by, instead of for, students.

7

Problem Finding and Problem Solving

"Figuring out what questions to ask will be more important than figuring out the answer," said Sam Altman, chief executive officer of OpenAI, the company behind ChatGPT (Stillman, 2025). He was talking about the future of AI and humanity. He predicts an economic transformation, and in the transformed economy, intelligence isn't the key to future success. "My kid is never going to grow up being smarter than AI," Altman noted. "The ability that will be valued is the ability to find problems and ask questions."

Teaching students to identify and solve problems is the key to future education (Zhao, 2022c) and should be the primary focus of education in the age of AI. It is also the primary rationale for personalizing learning.

Problem Finding

Personalization of learning can conform to traditional pedagogy, in which students follow online courses and instructors or use AI to learn content. This merely teaches students to be collectors of information, a worthless exercise in the age of AI when information is easily available. What should drive students' search for information is the need to solve problems they identify or answer questions they raise so that they can create new solutions to new problems and new answers to new questions.

Understanding why matters. Human beings are driven by purpose and meaning. Traditional schooling and the mandated curriculum are not designed to help students develop a sense of purpose. Even "career education" typically isn't about finding your purpose or even about discovering your meaning. It's about finding a job that fits your interests and helping you develop the skills and knowledge you need specifically for that job.

When students are given autonomy through personalized learning, they're much more likely to find questions and problems that matter to them and others. This is the crucial first step in personalized learning. Schools and teachers seem more interested in having students find answers than find questions. This is evident in the popular project-based learning (PBL) practices in schools. Although they are intended to promote inquiry-based learning and authentic problem solving, too often students play a relatively passive role in identifying the *P* in PBL. Usually, teachers decide on the problem to solve, and students are asked to come up with a solution. Even when students are asked to find problems, teachers are often tempted to quickly accept whatever problem or question students raise and move on to finding answers, without probing why the students chose the problem or question they did.

We cannot expect students to come up with the best problems or questions on the first try. As educators, our job is to help them expand their thinking and consider multiple perspectives. We want students to come up with a genuine problem, conduct research on it, refine it, seek feedback from the teacher and peers about it, and further refine it. It's an iterative process that can go through multiple rounds.

This is similar to the process that doctoral students go through in attempting to write dissertations. About half of PhD candidates in the United States do not complete their dissertations and finish their doctoral program (Council of Graduate Schools, 2008). This is often because students can't find a meaningful, compelling question. Many spend years trying to find it. When doctoral students propose their question, their professors often ask, "Why?" The first part of the dissertation is often about exactly that.

A venture capital investor from Silicon Valley once told me that they typically ask three questions of people seeking funding: Why? Why you? Why now? As for the first "why," it's easy to come up with a problem or question, but identifying *why* it actually matters is not so easy. In other words, who cares? Because we want students to engage in meaningful work, they must have reasons to believe the problem or question matters to someone. We want students to learn how to conduct research to find out if the problem has significance, and, if so, in what ways? We also want students to learn what evidence matters in convincing others of the importance of that problem.

Students can obtain evidence in different ways, depending on their questions. Some students may target a local problem—for example, a traffic light on a certain street that does not work well. In this case, they can conduct observations, surveys, and interviews and possibly obtain data from local governments to justify the need to fix the traffic light. Some students may find problems on a broader scale—for example, people's habits that cause water waste. They can go online and conduct research about the importance of water conservation and different ways to help people change their habits.

Students may have to abandon their problem or question if they are unable to find evidence to support its relevance. They could also dive deeper into the problem and find an underlying issue that is more significant. For example, students may initially raise the problem of peers wasting food at lunch in the school cafeteria, but on closer examination they may come to realize that the real problem is not that students are exhibiting the poor behavior of not finishing their food. Instead, the problem has to do with the low quality of the food. So instead of finding a solution to help their friends finish their food, they switch to solving the problem of improving the food quality.

Students should be encouraged to refine their problems and questions. They need to engage in conversations that provide meaningful feedback. Providing insightful feedback is different from evaluation. In fact, when students are given evaluative grades or comments, they view the job as completed and no longer feel compelled to revise or refine their work.

Students should always present their found problem or question to their peers. Public presentations, with parents, the school community, and people relevant to the problem in attendance, are a great way to generate feedback. Not only do students have to organize the presentation with valid and reliable evidence, but they must also learn to communicate with diverse audiences. Seeking feedback from the audience enables students to improve their questions and problems.

The second question—"Why you?"—is also important for students to answer. Why do you think *you* can solve this problem or answer the question? Can *you* solve it better than others? Is *your* answer an improvement over previous ones?

To answer this question, students will need to consider the resources they have. These could include their abilities, interests, personality, knowledge, and skills, as well as other qualities, such as attitudes and perspectives. They might also include resources they could receive externally, such as help from friends and families. Thinking about resources helps students ground their problem or question in reality and also promotes collaboration.

The third question—"Why now?"—pushes students to think about the importance of timing. Some problems may have been pertinent 50 years ago but have become less so today. Other questions may have had significance before certain technologies were invented, but now they no longer make sense. Some questions may be of great significance now, but given the resources available today, we cannot answer them yet.

Examples of how influential people find and refine problems can inspire students. Teachers could share short videos or stories of people who have solved meaningful problems, following it up with a discussion about the problem-finding process. They might also invite people who have come up with such solutions into the classroom to discuss the process with students. These can be ordinary, everyday people; they don't need to be famous.

Although design thinking has become popular in schools (Rowe, 1991), I would not recommend it for all students. It's a useful approach to finding and solving some—but not all—problems. Some pursuits, such as creating music, dance, and art or writing fiction and poetry, need more intuitive creativity than design thinking.

Creating High-Quality Works

I have two problems with the PBL practices I have observed. The first, as I noted, is that students usually are solving problems defined by the teacher. The second has to do with the mindset—the process of PBL typically matters more than the products (Zhao, 2012, 2016d). Students must care about the final product because they are real problem solvers. They want to produce authentic products that matter to the world.

Students' authentic work can often surprise adults, because many adults don't think students are capable of producing such high-quality products. I've seen many student-produced PowerPoint presentations, videos, and works of music and art. There are some impressive products, for sure. At High Tech High in San Diego, California, students produced excellent artwork, books, and videos that they proudly marketed to the public (Zhao, 2012). But this is the exception.

Adults must first believe that students *can* produce high-quality products. We have seen countless examples of students doing just that. Greta Thunberg started her climate activism at age 15, and Malala Yousafzai became the youngest Nobel Prize winner at age 17 for her advocacy work for women's education. At age 11, Gitanjali Rao developed Tethys, a device using carbon nanotube sensors to detect lead in drinking water. These young people saw big problems and devoted themselves to solving them. (For more examples, see McDiarmid et al., 2025.)

Most students have not had the experience of solving meaningful problems that have a real impact on their lives. They need accomplishments and encouragement, as well as specific constructive feedback. But more important, they need to learn to *objectify* their proposed problems and solutions. Objectification puts a distance between the creator and the created so that feedback, especially feedback that points out areas of improvement, can be more readily accepted. Some people have trouble accepting constructive feedback and easily become defensive because they associate their egos too closely with their ideas. If we can learn to make ideas, even our own ideas, objects in the world, we can add distance between self and objects. This makes it easier for us to change our minds when we realize our ideas are wrong.

The process of improving product quality is the same as refining questions. It's an iterative process: We get feedback, we revise the solution, we get more feedback, and we revise some more. This is similar to the continuous improvement cycle that many businesses have employed as advocated by Edward Deming (Petersen, 1999). But even high-quality products are not perfect products. No matter how hard we try and how many times we revise, we can always improve the product. It's important for students to see their products released to the public, but they need to learn to release them only after they reach a certain quality level and with the understanding that the product can always be improved later on.

Collaboration is typically necessary for creating high-quality solutions or finding high-quality answers. Some products do not necessarily require collaboration, such as writing fiction or poetry. But producing a novel would require it. The author generally needs editing, cover design, promotion, and possibly the inclusion of photos or graphics.

Finding and solving problems should not be about having all members of the team doing the same work or duplicating one another's work. It requires a productive division of labor based on the project's needs and individuals' interests and strengths, rather like in an orchestra.

Some students will abandon their problems or questions and join other students to work on a different topic. The process of collaboratively finding and solving problems requires students to convince colleagues to accept their ideas and join their team. Teachers and students can decide how many projects the class can handle, and, therefore, how many ideas to pursue. Not all ideas will make the cut.

Using AI to Find and Solve Problems

AI can play a significant role in the process of learning to find and solve problems. To start with, students can brainstorm questions or problems, asking AI for feedback and suggestions. They can also ask for examples. They can use AI to conduct research about their proposed problems or even to suggest questions to jump-start their thinking. AI can also create presentations, develop project timelines, produce images and videos, and generate music.

AI can serve as a tutor or teacher to help students learn new knowledge and develop new skills as they find, refine, and address various problems and solutions. Instead of thinking about developing AI literacy courses for students to help them in this work, we should, instead, just give them time to work and play with AI. When they have a concrete objective, they will develop personalized approaches to interacting with AI through the work experience.

Students should treat AI as a partner in finding and solving problems. In a sense, students and AI are in a co-evolutionary relationship—that is, in a relationship between human beings and technology (Bruno, 2022; Donati, 2021; Lee, 2020). The basic idea is simple: Human beings and technology mutually influence each other. Humans make technological changes, which then change human beings, who then make more changes in technology, which further affect human beings. This brings to mind Winston Churchill's saying "We shape our buildings; thereafter they shape us," except that the process I'm referring to is ongoing.

AI is rapidly developing, with new capabilities and functions emerging all the time. We do not know what AI will eventually become, but given AI functions today, we know that students could offload many tasks to AI systems to focus on finding and solving problems. The more students use AI for meaningful purposes, the more likely they will understand it better and use it more intelligently. Then AI will co-evolve to become a more personalized partner for students.

In Sum

Finding problems and questions that matter is one of the most valuable skills in the age of AI. However, the traditional prescribed curriculum in schools usually only teaches known answers to known questions or problems. In this chapter, we discussed a different approach: how to help students find and refine problems and questions, as well as make high-quality products.

As students research their questions and problems, they make connections among different theories, phenomena, people, and the world's realities. Students need to see and take advantage of opportunities. In many ways, finding and solving just the right problem seems to require luck, but luck is simply preparedness and courage when opportunities arise.

8

Human Interdependence and Global Competence

Less than 10 years ago, global competence was a hot topic. There were numerous calls for schools to prepare their students to be globally competent (Reimers, 2008). Governments wanted their students to be globally competent. Organizations such as the Asia Society (2008) led the development of the content of global competencies, and international tests such as PISA even included an assessment of the global competence of 15-year-old students in different countries in 2018 (OECD, 2018). International study tours; global exchanges of students and teachers, online and offline (Lindsay & Davis, 2012); joint global projects in teaching and research, as well as publications and conferences on global competence, were all on the rise in the world.

But today, global competence has all but disappeared from the conversation. What happened?

Many things, in fact, and the world has changed. The COVID-19 pandemic has affected every aspect of human life. The Russia-Ukraine war and the Israel-Hamas conflicts have forced people and countries to regroup politically, economically, and militarily. Gaping ideological divides in many countries have resulted in intense political and cultural conflict. Trade wars between countries have redefined international relationships, and long-standing international organizations and agreements have been challenged and reshaped. And generative AI tools, such as ChatGPT, have emerged. These changes have generated both profound fear and hope across the world. The "flat world" that Thomas Friedman (2007) predicted in his bestseller, *The World Is Flat: A Brief History of the Twenty-First Century*, failed to materialize.

In this new world of divisions, conflicts, and wars, interest in global competence nearly disappeared from educational agendas. Local problems have overwhelmed education systems and schools. Among these were teacher and administrator shortages, as well as the need to address perceived lost learning during the pandemic. There were also political conflicts, such as book bans and baseless concerns about "critical race theory," "furries," and litter boxes in classrooms. Added to the mix was the issue of regulating students' use of smartphones in classrooms. Little wonder that educators have not had time to think beyond dealing with the most recent crisis—real or manufactured—much less rethink the education we actually need today.

Technology enables learning beyond the classroom. Yet most students are still isolated in their physical classrooms, with few opportunities for authentic interactions—face-to-face or virtual—with people beyond their classes, schools, communities, or countries. As a result, we are failing to help our students learn to live well with others. This helps us understand why many citizens in different countries elect or choose to obey extreme politicians who become popular by fomenting hatred toward people who they perceive are not like them. Current education is not helping students understand that human beings, regardless of location, are mutually interdependent. Malicious intentions to demonize the "other" to gain power often backfire, as history has repeatedly shown.

Human Interdependence

Personalized learning is intended to provide people with the autonomy they need to develop their strengths and interests so that they can realize their potential (Zhao, 2018b, 2018c, 2023). Personalization enables students to realize their strengths and value by finding and solving significant problems. Through this process, individuals come to understand that their value lies in using their abilities to serve others (Seligman, 2002; Zhao, 2012). In serving others, they reach self-actualization and authentic happiness.

Although personalization encourages the cultivation of interests and the development of strengths, it also encourages individuals to not spend time and energy on tasks for which they lack aptitude. No one can be good at everything. Everyone has weaknesses, which presents opportunities for others to offer help with their own strengths and interests. It's all about human interdependence.

Human interdependence underlies the concept of the division of labor. In the 18th century, numerous scholars, such as Adam Smith (1776/2016), discussed how the division of labor enhanced economic productivity. In the 19th century, French philosopher Emile Durkheim (1893/2014), in his book *The Division of Labor in Society,* argued that the benefits of the division of labor extend beyond economic efficiency; they also contribute to the social and moral order.

Nevertheless, this phenomenon of the division of labor has rarely been applied in schools. Students learn about the idea in economics yet seldom experience it in practice. Schools treat students as independent individuals following the same pathways, learning largely the same content, and developing similar skills. Few schools teach students to depend on one another while developing at the same time different capabilities based on their interests and personal strengths. Students may learn about interdependence and the division of labor in team sports, but team sports are not mainstream curricular activities.

Tracking (Terrin & Triventi, 2023) has been practiced in many schools, and it does seem to provide students with different courses and content. However, it's largely based on students' academic performance instead of on their interests and strengths. Students are also placed in different tracks that are typically preset by schools; the students themselves have no choice in this placement.

Even when schools teach collaboration, the focus is on the collaborative skills one needs and the strategies one should use, rather than on human interdependence. Human interdependence is based on the fact that we all have different strengths, weaknesses, and interests, that we can work to improve our strengths, that we should accept we can be weak in certain areas, and that we can use our strengths to create value for others as we let others create value for us.

Human interdependence explains why diversity improves resilience and productivity in groups and institutions (Page, 2007). If we truly believe in human interdependence, we teachers should be helping students to understand their strengths and to work out how they can use their strengths to create value for others. Students should be encouraging their peers to do the same. Further, we want them to look at the people around them to find opportunities to apply their strengths. In essence, it helps to think about how, together, we could make the entire team or organization work better, instead of looking down at others because they do not have the talents and qualities we think they should have.

This is the foundation of true collaboration. It relies on the diversity of perspectives, interests, and talents, as well as on mutual respect. Thus, teaching collaboration is not about collaborative skills or strategies. Rather, it's about social intelligence (Zhao, 2016a), which is the ability to understand others, know their strengths and interests, know who can help with what, and know when help is needed.

The Selfish School

Human interdependence drives students to use their strengths and interests to solve problems for others, instead of competing against one another. Traditional schools typically force students to be selfish through manufactured competition. In every class, students are ranked on the basis of their performance; *A*s, *B*s, or *F*s indicate one's standing. Even the supposedly more innovative assessments, such as no grades or rubric-based assessments that are criteria-referenced, still tell students whether they have exceeded or failed to meet the standards. Standardized tests, whether state-mandated or voluntary, such as the SAT or ACT, do the same. College admissions often rely on students' SAT/ACT scores, their grade point averages, and class rankings.

This means that students must outperform their peers to advance to the next level or to qualify for admission to a prestigious institution. In this system, when someone is on the top, someone else has to be at the bottom. Those who rank at the top can be very happy and receive all sorts of opportunities, whereas those at the bottom are often deprived of such opportunities. The competition in schools can be fierce, especially in those schools that aim to prepare students for elite colleges. Academic pressure largely comes from this competition.

Productive human interdependence would look quite different. Instead of having a single scale of capabilities, it would include numerous, unlimited scales that could measure the diversity of human capabilities. In fact, any unique capability can have its own scale. Even math abilities can have a variety of scales (e.g., theoretical math, practical math, geometry, or probability). On some, a student may rank near the top, whereas on others, they may rank near the bottom. In this scenario, students would focus on using their strengths to find and solve problems for others, instead of competing against others. We know that as biological beings, humans are self-interested, which is not the same as being selfish. Selfishness is shortsighted and can come at any cost, ignoring long-term outcomes or the impact on others. Self-interest can be altruistic; it may entail using one's strengths and interests to serve others.

From Human Interdependence to Global Competency

Human conflicts arise for several reasons. Competition for limited resources is a major factor. Humans compete for land and water, to gain a spot in an elite college, to rise to a higher position in an organization—and they often turn to violence in the process. Conflicting cultural, ideological, and religious beliefs are another source of clashes, especially when one group wishes to impose its beliefs on others. Inequalities in the distribution of power and resources within societies marginalize or victimize some groups. Over time, conflicts occur as the marginalized groups seek to redress injustices.

Evolutionary and psychological factors play a role as well. From an evolutionary point of view, cooperation has been essential for human survival, but competition and aggression have also shaped the process. From a psychological perspective, human individuals tend to align with groups to which they feel an affinity, sometimes because the group offers protection from the "other." Here, fear, mistrust, and the need for belonging and identity contribute to conflict.

Numerous researchers from a wide range of academic fields—economics, psychology, anthropology, political science, and sociology, to name a few—have studied these factors. Yet most schools have done little to help students develop a more rational approach to peace and conflict, nor have we learned much about how to teach them to work toward bringing peace and prosperity for all. Some schools have taught peace education (Harris, 2004) and conflict resolution (Johnson & Johnson, 1996), but these initiatives remain marginal. One researcher (Jones, 2004) reported that 18–24 percent of public schools offered conflict resolution training. It's unclear whether these programs help students understand how they can realize their self-interests through helping others.

The concept of human interdependence not only addresses human conflict on the individual level but also can serve as the core concept of global competence. Although there are various definitions of global competence (e.g., see the Council on International Education Exchange, 1988; Hunter et al., 2006; OECD, 2018; Reimers, 2010; University of Wisconsin-Global Competence Task Force, 2008), no one definition has generally been accepted. PISA defined it as "the capacity to examine local, global, and intercultural issues, to understand and appreciate the perspectives and world views of others, to engage in open, appropriate, and effective interactions with people from different cultures, and to act for collective well-being and sustainable development" (OECD, 2018). Harvard professor Fernando Reimers (2010) defined it as a positive disposition toward cultural differences and a framework of global values, a proficiency in multiple languages, and a deep knowledge and understanding of world affairs.

These definitions may sound reasonable, but they are not practical. They are overly reliant on information about others. Students would need to be taught about multiple perspectives, cultures, values, and languages. Given the diversity and number of cultures and languages globally, such an undertaking would be impossible. Moreover, global competence doesn't just mean knowing about the diverse cultures across the world. It also means dealing with local issues that are, in fact, global, such as climate change; immigration; and regulating potentially threatening technologies, such as foreign social media apps.

Elsewhere, I have proposed that global competence include the understanding of interdependence and interconnectedness (Zhao, 2009). This means caring about the shared fate of human beings. We're forever interconnected and interdependent in all aspects of humanity. Marshall McLuhan's global village is no longer in the future and is even richer than he imagined in the 1960s. Not only do villagers know quite a bit about other villagers, thanks to electronic media, but also the lives of global villagers are profoundly affected by the actions of others. For example, when I went back to my remote village in China, I found that the villagers' lives were closely connected to the outside world. They watch news about the United States, use cell phone chips invented overseas, drive American or Japanese cars, and work at factories that export products to the United States. In contrast, I hardly knew that the United States was a country when I grew up there.

Malicious politicians may invade other countries, launch trade wars, disrupt global alliances, deport immigrants, disrupt air travel, and close borders. Keep in mind, also, that the COVID-19 pandemic didn't need a passport to travel and that extreme weather conditions don't respect borders. These are reminders that we only have one Earth and that anyone, anywhere on this globe, can do damage to it.

Instead of teaching students more narrowly about various cultures, geographies, and religions, teaching human interdependence through personalization and problem finding and problem solving would be a more natural learning process for developing global competence. By weaving this concept into daily schoolwork, we would have a world of citizens who care about themselves but who also work on making the world a better place. By bettering the world and others, we all become better ourselves.

Knowing Your Audience

Students need to develop a sense of audience to understand who they are and what problems or questions are worth tackling. Students could conduct surveys or interviews with potential audiences. Even those students who are interested in artistic work, such as poetry, painting, fiction, or music, should develop a sense of their potential audience.

Students also need to consider their audience in both local and global terms. Local problems or questions may involve their classes, schools, or issues their friends may have. Students should also go beyond their schools and look for problems and questions in their communities, villages, or neighborhoods. Most important for developing global competence, we want our students to think about other countries and the world.

For example, I was involved in an experimental program in Chongqing, China—the Innovation, Creativity, and Entrepreneurship Education program, which implements personalized learning and problem finding and solving in the middle school. The students who volunteered to join the program asked to conduct research and develop materials for promoting tourism in the city. The overall problem offered students many smaller problems to solve. For example, they could look at the "hot treasures" of the city—new emerging ones, where older ones were, and whether those older ones were in the process of disappearing or had already disappeared. They could also examine problems in transportation, architecture, lifestyle, food, and other aspects of the city that would be of interest to tourists. Most important, the students interacted with students in other countries to seek their views of tourism and to solicit feedback.

In Sum

Global competence is crucial today, given the fact that we live in a world divided by politics, greediness, misinformation, distrust, fear, and inequality. Nevertheless, we all want the younger generation to live a better life, in peace and prosperity. Schools should not isolate themselves from the outside world, nor should they isolate their students from knowledge about global conflicts and the deterioration of the earth. Teaching global competence doesn't mean teaching students about the myriad cultures, foreign languages, histories, or religions. Rather, it is about helping students understand how humans are interconnected and interdependent and how, through personalized learning, we can use our interests and strengths to help others and improve our world.

9

The School Within a School: A New Approach to Educational Transformation

I have on numerous occasions presented these ideas—the personalization of learning based on interests and strengths, teaching students to find and solve problems for others, and developing human interdependence—at conferences and workshops to teachers, school leaders, and policymakers in education. These ideas were always well received. But few believed that schools could actually implement them.

After trying to improve how to cut string beans in a hotel in his teenage years, Nobel prize-winning physicist Richard Feynman (1985) noted, "I learned there that innovation is a very difficult thing in the real world" (p. 29). Improving schools has defied reformers for decades. Scholars have cited a long list of reasons to explain why, including complex systems, wrong-headed policymakers, change-averse teachers, ineffective school leaders, obstructive parents, ill-conceived curricula, inadequate facilities and resources, and so on.

Failed Education and Education Reforms

One could look at this list and throw up their hands. But I respond differently. Significant changes *must* happen because education is failing to prepare students for today's world, let alone for tomorrow's. Numerous scholars, government agencies, and international organizations have been calling for the teaching of new skills and abilities for the new century. As yet, we have little evidence that schools have changed enough to teach those skills. More seriously, the skills students *are* being taught don't match today's rapidly changing job market. Millions of U.S. students graduate from high school and college but fail to land a high-paying job (U.S. Bureau of Labor Statistics, 2024). The situation will worsen with the rapid development in AI. In the meantime, we have businesses complaining that they cannot find the talents they need. Further, when AI and technology take away existing jobs, they also create new jobs. Graduates need to be prepared for those.

However, predicting what knowledge and skills will be important in the future is increasingly difficult. Many of the jobs in most demand today didn't exist 15 years ago—for example, AI and machine learning specialists, data scientists and analysts, and social media managers (McDiarmid & Zhao, 2022). Thus, there is no guarantee that what students learn in schools today will help them thrive in the future.

Might education systems and schools relax the curriculum and give some opportunities for students to personalize their learning so that they can develop skills that could be important in the future? Some schools are on this path. Innovative schools such as Summerhill in the United Kingdom (Neil, 1960) and Sudbury Valley School in the United States (Greenberg et al., 2005) offer tremendous autonomy to students (Zhao, 2012). Democratic schools (Apple & Beane, 1995; Chamberlin, 1989) have also been in existence for quite a long time and have been studied by education researchers. Montessori schools (Montessori, 1912/2013) exist in various forms and places, as do Dalton schools (Jackman, 1920). In recent years, other innovative schools have come into being that practice personalized learning and project-based learning, such as High Tech High schools in San Diego, California

(Wagner & Dintersmith, 2015) and Big Picture schools in various parts of the world (Washor et al., 2021).

An Interesting Success and Failure

Bill McDiarmid, former dean of education at the University of North Carolina at Chapel Hill, told me a fascinating but unfortunate story about an education experiment that happened about 40 years ago. The story was also recounted in an article written by one of the participating English teachers, David Donavel (1995).

In September 1989, Masconomet Regional High School in Massachusetts implemented a different approach to schooling. Half of its students chose to attend the traditional program (Tradpro), and the other half chose to attend a new school, called the Renaissance Program (Renpro). Renpro was conceived by the superintendent and designed by nine teachers during the summer. Renpro differed significantly from the traditional program in that the school year was divided into three trimesters of 60 days. Students took two classes each trimester, and each class was 100 minutes long (later 118 minutes). The heart of the program was different time allocation and block scheduling. Renpro essentially became a school within a school.

The program was evaluated by a group of researchers from Harvard University. The group found that although students at Tradpro had better academic performance at the beginning of the year than those who chose Renpro, by the end of the year, the Renpro students did better in almost every aspect: academic achievement in school subjects, problem solving, and writing. More important, Renpro students enjoyed their classes and school more and had more positive social and emotional states. In short, Renpro was a huge success.

But success did not help Renpro spread to the entire school. The school committee seemed to dislike success. They voted to discontinue the program in October 1990 because the program was controversial. According to Donavel, "The 'official' reason for the decision was that the school district needed to pass an override of Proposition 2 1/2, a Massachusetts state law that caps local tax increases, and that the likelihood of doing so with the controversial Renpro in the school was small" (1995, p. 6).

This story interests me because it tells me that anyone can change and can make change happen. The superintendent and a few teachers started the Renpro program; it didn't take extra resources, funding, or facilities. It did not take anything away from other teachers or the school. The changes seemed easy to make.

But changes are fragile. They can easily be undone, especially when the innovator departs or if the changes challenge the existing status quo. According to Donavel, the parents of students in the traditional school didn't like the fact that their children's rankings were challenged by students in Renpro, who likely succeeded as well as they did because of the innovative program.

Change Starts with You

Current educational systems are unlikely to initiate and lead the needed shift. Practicing educators should not wait for systems or "reformers" to bring about change. Instead, they should do it themselves, whenever possible and at whatever scale they can. The more people are making changes, the more likely change will occur on a large scale. This may sound quixotic, but individual students, teachers, and school leaders have brought about change, as the following research project I led shows.

In 2018, a group of doctoral students in a class I taught at the University of Kansas conducted research about transformational change in classes and schools. The students conducted research about students, teachers, and school leaders who have implemented personalized learning and finding and solving problems for others. See *An Education Crisis Is a Terrible Thing to Waste: How Radical Changes Can Spark Student Excitement and Success* (Zhao et al., 2019).

We found that many teachers made big changes in their classes. Some enabled students to run businesses, offer services to others, and become entrepreneurs; others gave students time for passion projects, where they could exercise autonomy and become responsible for their own learning; and still others assisted students to venture into areas where their school lacked needed resources and expertise. These teachers made changes because they were tired of teaching in the traditional way, they wanted to see a better future for their students, and they wanted to help meet students' needs for more autonomy.

School leaders can bring about big change as well. Peter Hutton (2022), former principal of Templestowe College, Australia, tells about how he turned a troubled school into a flourishing one through personalization of learning and engaging students in entrepreneurial activities in which they found and solved authentic problems. School leaders of a network of independent schools and public schools in South Australia and other places also made significant changes to their schools to enable personalization and entrepreneurial learning.

Students can also bring about change. A group of students, led by Sam Levin, a high school student at Monument Mountain Regional High School in Great Barrington, Massachusetts, started the Independent Project in 2010. This student-run program aimed at fostering personalized learning (Levin & Engel, 2016). The project was a wild success, and others have tried to copy it, although with limited success due to administrative constraints (Lane, 2018).

Over the past decade, I have been working with schools in Australia, China, and the United States to help them make transformative changes. Two groups of public schools in Australia's states of Victoria and New South Wales, under the sponsorship of the Mitchell Institute of Victoria University in 2016, participated in the project. Each group had about 10 schools that were willing to participate. The schools ranged from high-performing suburban schools to struggling schools in rural areas. Schools organized teams of voluntary students, led by one or two voluntary teachers, to participate in this experiment, which we called Paradigm Shifters. Schools typically devoted one course to personalization and problem finding and solving. The project lasted a year. The evaluation report (Anderson et al., 2017) showed that the project improved students' self-agency, engagement with schools, and entrepreneurial thinking.

Prisoners of Imagination

Why do we seem unable to change education? Being "prisoners of our imaginations" is usually to blame. In Jean-Paul Sartre's play *No Exit*, the characters—Garcin, Inès, and Estelle—find themselves in a room in Hell. They're ensnared by their own perceptions, desires, and the relentless judgments of one another. This self-imposed imprisonment illustrates how individuals can become captives of their own minds, constrained by their imaginations and the meanings they assign to their experiences.

We are, in some way, all prisoners of our own imagination. When I talk to school leaders about change, most of them invariably imagine that it's the controlling power of the system that prevents them from making significant changes to the curriculum. However, there are no curricular police from the education system who come to classrooms to inspect whether the curriculum is being implemented exactly as prescribed. Without any evidence, school leaders also imagine that students and parents will oppose the changes. But as the Masconomet Regional High School's Renaissance project showed, half of the students—and presumably their families—were interested in the transformational change.

Talking to system leaders, they always tell me they want innovative school leaders to make significant changes, and they claim that the system requirements are not about control. They're only there, they say, to provide support. In the absence of change, they may imagine that their school leaders are incompetent or lazy, either unwilling or unable to bring about change. This assumption is, of course, incorrect (Watterston & Zhao, 2024).

Teachers also are prisoners of their own imagination. They could be trapped by what they imagine are their students' interests, motivations, and abilities. They could also be trapped by what they imagine to be their colleagues' attitudes, perspectives, teaching styles and capabilities, as well as their view of relationships. Further, they could be trapped by what they imagine to be their leaders' perspectives on students, educational change, teacher evaluation, and teaching outcomes. There are even more traps of imagination, such as the time they might have to spend in making changes and whether they even have the ability to do so.

To break out of the prison of our own imaginings, we first need to examine our imaginations. If we probe the thinking of the people we have imaginings about, we may be surprised how wrong we are about what *we* think *they* think. We could also simply collect data by asking students and parents how much they like the school or class and whether they would like to see changes. We could also propose changes and present them to the relevant people to see how they respond.

The Potential of the School Within a School

What I wish for is speedy and large-scale changes in the entire education system globally so that all students can engage in personalizable education to develop their interests and strengths through finding and solving problems for others and the world (McDiarmid & Zhao, 2022; Zhao, 2018b, 2018c, 2023). But I understand this is impossible. So I have moderated my expectations and hopes, advocating for and supporting transformational changes that teachers, students, and school leaders can make on a smaller scale. I can summarize these smaller-scale changes as a school-within-a-school (SwS) model.

Schools have always run special programs. These include traditional tracking programs that put different students in different courses (Terrin & Triventi, 2023), talented and gifted programs, special education programs, and autonomous school-within-a-school programs in elementary and secondary schools. The SwS model has been defined as "large public schools that have been divided into smaller autonomous subunits" and "a separate entity, running its own budget and planning its own programs" (McAndrews, 2002, p. 2). SwS does not necessarily need to run its own budget, but it should be able to plan its own programs.

I am suggesting SwS as a way forward to implement the transformational changes needed in education for several reasons. First, it is quite difficult to convince the entire staff, students, and parents of a school that significant changes are needed (Dolph, 2017). Even when people are convinced of change, they may not want the proposed transformational change. Educators should be invited to participate in innovative initiatives, rather than having initiatives imposed on them. In every school, some students are not being well served and some teachers want change. These can be the first group of innovators.

Second, many schools have market pressure. They are worried about their reputation to attract students. That is, they do not want to lose their students because of the change. Creating a new school or program within the school essentially diversifies the school's educational offerings, which can better meet the needs of a diverse student population, without touching the original school's tradition or reputation.

Third, and perhaps most important, every community a school serves has students and parents who want something different from what the existing school offers. No school that offers just a single educational experience serves all students well. Underserved, disaffected, or marginalized students have no choice and are stuck in the school. The same is true for teachers. No matter how well teachers are trained, there are dissatisfied teachers who would like to teach differently. Building a school within a school offers these teachers and students an option.

In Sum

Although many scholars have discussed why schools cannot change and why changes are hard to sustain, we have also seen multiple examples of transformational changes. Although such changes may not last long, they may have a lasting effect on some students and teachers. So, instead of wishing for systems to adopt policies for radical change, I propose that everyone in the education system—students, teachers, school leaders, policymakers, and even parents—is capable of making meaningful changes. Perhaps the most feasible approach in schools today is the school-within-a-school model. My goal is to see more schools experiment with such an approach.

10

Where to Go from Here

What prompted me to think about writing this book is the release of the 2022 PISA results (OECD, 2023). I was deeply struck by the observed decline in student performance in all three subjects (math, reading, and science) *across OECD countries* since the start of PISA. Earlier, I was equally struck by the lack of significant progress in reading and math of 9- and 13-year-olds in NAEP's long-term assessment from the 1970s to 2020s (NAEP, 2021). I had mistakenly believed this was only a U.S. problem.

I don't believe that test scores reflect the total quality of education, and I have been critical of PISA's claim that it measures the knowledge and skills needed in the 21st century (Zhao, 2016e, 2020b, 2024). But whatever PISA measures, the OECD has encouraged governments globally to learn lessons from high PISA performers, such as Finland and Shanghai. Numerous publications and commentors have urged policymakers to adopt instructional materials from these high-performing countries. Bevies of policymakers and educators have made pilgrimages to and teacher exchanges with these alleged exemplars. Some countries, keen to raise their students' scores, have changed their educational policies to align with those of the higher performers. Researchers have studied PISA results in the hopes of teasing out the "secret sauce" behind successful countries. Yet, if this global focus on the policies and practices of high performers was warranted, PISA scores should not have slipped.

The NAEP data are equally puzzling. After decades of reforms and billions of dollars invested to improve reading and math, why are so many students' reading skills no better today than the reading skills of students in 1992? And why have math skills improved only marginally, with high performers accounting for most of the improvement?

Many explanations are offered: student demographic changes, economic upturns and downturns, technological advances, social media, mobile devices, and possible changes in or instability of the tests. Other explanations include family relations, community shifts, immigration, "wokeness," and political divisions. Whatever the explanation, the reality is that we have not seen significant sustained improvement in the test scores in the core school subjects over the past three and a half decades.

Significant Reforms Versus Transformational Changes

One of the biggest contributors to the lack of progress is the massive reforms that many countries have undertaken and that PISA has encouraged. These reforms—for example, NCLB in the United States; the National Assessment Program: Literacy and Numeracy (NAPLAN) implementation in Australia; the use of Shanghai math in England; and Germany's introduction of national education standards and additional assessments after the "PISA shock" in 2000—have all had an impact on schools and changed school cultures. It is not an exaggeration to say that these reforms were "significant."

Their significance stems, however, from reforms that strengthen the past instead of creating alternatives for the future. The significant government-dictated reforms have reinforced the dominant paradigm of education: state-mandated, standardized curriculum and assessment; increased student time spent on the required curriculum; greater focus of teacher training on teaching the required curriculum; and increased accountability for school leaders to implement the prescribed curriculum. In other words, none of the reforms led to meaningful changes in schools but only enhanced the traditional paradigm of schooling (Zhao & Zhong, 2024).

Schools need meaningful changes. Schools have been declared broken, ineffective, or outdated for a long time because they have failed to address the needs of each student or support each student to realize their potential. Schools have also failed to keep pace with rapid advances in technology (Goldin & Katz, 2008). Reforms put a bandage on fundamental problems and merely tinker with the components of the grammar of schooling in the hope of achieving utopia (Tyack & Cuban, 1995).

The changes may be significant, but they do not truly transform schools. This new age requires different talents, abilities, knowledge, and mindsets. Traditional schooling cannot be improved to cultivate these new requirements, any more than a horse-drawn wagon can be improved to get us to the moon or Mars. Similarly, traditional schooling can neither equitably nor effectively address the disparate needs of the diversity of students in our schools.

Nothing Works for Everyone

The history of education is a history of jumping from one surefire remedy to the next. Every few years, a new idea comes along and becomes popular. It becomes the latest buzz at conferences, workshops, and professional development programs. Schools and teachers jump on these ideas, hoping they will address the ills in their schools. School financial resources and teachers' time and energy focus on learning about these ideas with the hope they will be applied in the classroom.

Initially, we typically hear reports on how these remedies are producing remarkable results. These initial success stories are often used to promote and spread the idea until some less positive stories come out. As more and more classrooms and schools implement the idea, enthusiasm begins to flag. Some schools and teachers begin to find that some students do not benefit from the initiative and that some may even get hurt by it. Even as this latest great idea fades from the stage, a new one makes its entrance. There are always folks at work on the next cure-all, especially when there's money to be made.

As I have argued throughout this book, the reality is that most educational interventions work for some students, but no intervention works for all students all the time. Research (and common sense) has for some time shown that students are differently talented and have different types of intelligence (Gardner, 1983). Recent research about neurodiversity suggests that students have a wide range of neurological differences, encompassing variations in attention, learning, mood, and socialization preferences. We need to recognize that such differences are natural variations in human cognition, rather than deficits, disorders, or instructional inconveniences (Armstrong, 2012; Ellis et al., 2023).

Consider, also, family conditions. Physical location, for example, significantly contributes to student diversity. Born and raised in Manhattan is drastically different from born and raised in a small town in Alaska. Social and economic status condition brain development, physical development, social and emotional development, as well as academic learning, adding even more diversity (Lechner et al., 2021; Liu et al., 2022; Rakesh & Whittle, 2021; Suglia et al., 2022). And then there are those additional factors, such as race, religion, immigration status, and cultural values.

The idea of "nature via nurture" tells the powerful journey of how innate human nature interacts with one's experiences and conditions to create uniquely different human beings (Ridley, 2003). The "triple helix" proposed by the late Harvard evolutionary biologist Richard Lewontin (2001) explains the potentially random interactions among genes, organisms, and environment, which, again, creates more diversity.

It's therefore impossible to imagine that one intervention would apply to all students in all conditions. This is also why the numerous efforts to close the achievement gap (Hess, 2011) have not worked and why they won't work in the future (Hanushek et al., 2019). We should abandon the belief that some new surefire solution will appear. Instead, we should be imagining a new paradigm of education, especially in the age of AI.

Establishing a New Paradigm of Education

In his influential work *The Structure of Scientific Revolutions*, philosopher Thomas Kuhn (1962) discussed changes in scientific paradigms, such as the shift from Newtonian mechanics to Einstein's theory of relativity. In science, a *paradigm* is the overarching framework that encompasses the theories, methods, standards, and assumptions that define legitimate contributions to a particular field.

In education, we can borrow the concept and think about educational paradigm shifts, or educational revolutions. According to Kuhn, scientific progress occurs through a series of phases. In the pre-paradigm phase, there are diverse and competing theories without a unified framework; in the normal science phase, the scientific community operates within an accepted paradigm; in the crisis phase, there appears an accumulation of anomalies that the current paradigm cannot explain; then comes the paradigm shift phase, when a new paradigm emerges that better explains the anomalies. In the end, the new paradigm is established in the phase of new normal science.

The modern education paradigm has existed and been strengthened over the past 200-plus years since its inception in Prussia. Here are the accepted components of the theory: Students need to be taught by teachers in classrooms, test scores are the best measure of learning, curriculum and pedagogy should be standardized as much as possible, and policy and research should operate within and support the paradigm. Although anomalies have emerged, they have been dismissed.

I have shown that this paradigm of education has failed to help the majority of students reach their full potential. We know that students do not need teachers to learn; they can learn on their own through peer tutoring and technology. Most important, the outcomes—what we expect our students to know when they graduate—have changed. It is time to push for a paradigm shift in education.

Recently, diverse and competing alternative approaches to education—ones that have existed for centuries—have increased. These include small, online parent-run schools; schools within a school; student-run schools; personalized curriculum; project-based and problem-based learning; homeschooling; Montessori schools; Reggio programs; and a host of other educational institutions that change the role of teachers and students, redefine the meaning of schools (virtual as opposed to physical), and promise different outcomes. This is perhaps the pre-paradigm phase for education.

The new paradigm has not coalesced yet, but it will likely take into account the following:

- Students are more active, capable, and purpose-driven than we thought.
- Students have a jagged profile of capabilities, with strengths and weaknesses.
- The jaggedness of their profiles is precisely what we need in a world that has been largely transformed by technology.
- Students need more say in the curriculum.
- Finding and solving meaningful problems should be the main mode of learning because access to information is ubiquitous. Learning is much more than collecting information. It involves finding and answering questions.
- The role of teachers needs to change from knowledge instruction to facilitation and support.
- Learning must expand beyond physical classrooms and schools.
- Assessments need to be fundamentally rethought. Rather than a tool to rank and select students, assessments need to be tools for learning. (Zhong & Zhao, 2025)

Personalized Learning *Is* Possible

Learning has to be personalized. In medicine and healthcare, one fast-growing area is *personalized medicine* or *precision medicine,* an innovative approach that tailors medical treatment to the individual characteristics of each patient. Personalized medicine considers factors such as a person's genetic profile, environment, and lifestyle to guide decisions related to the prevention, diagnosis, and treatment of diseases. The ultimate goal of personalized medicine is to provide more precise, predictable, and effective healthcare that is customized for the individual patient and to move away from the traditional "one-size-fits-all" approach. Given the available science and technology, we can similarly personalize education.

The rapid development of AI has shocked the world. AI has already surpassed human beings in many areas, and artificial general intelligence (AGI)—a hypothetical form of artificial intelligence capable of performing any intellectual task that a human being can perform—may soon become a reality. In today's reality, generative AI has already become a powerful tool for numerous teachers and students. It has already developed into numerous AI-driven applications for students. These include personalized learning platforms such as Coursera, tutoring systems such as Iris, study aids such as Quizlet and Anki, writing tools such as Grammarly, math problem solvers such as Photomath and QANDA, and AI-powered learning communities such as Brainly. These AI-driven applications are all designed to cater to diverse learning needs, providing personalized support and enhancing the overall educational experience for students.

Along with the new AI-powered tools, the COVID-19 pandemic brought about a significant growth of online learning resources. These include video-based courses in every school subject, including physical education; tutoring materials; online tutors; quizzes and practice tests; and numerous Massive Open Online Courses (MOOCs) offered by colleges and experts, which give K–12 students access to more advanced content. The pandemic also revealed to teachers, students, and school leaders that online learning is both possible and, when done well, effective. The number of public online virtual schools has also grown. These online resources provide opportunities for students to personalize their learning, and they relieve schools of the need to offer courses in all subjects, especially more advanced ones (Zhao, 2022b).

Of course, other tools also support the personalization of learning. The digitization of publications has put practically the majority of human products online, even those dating back thousands of years. This includes books, journals, magazines, newspapers, music, art works, and films. Many museums and art galleries have also begun digitizing their collections and putting them online. Google Maps and other mapping tools cover noteworthy places (both buildings and natural scenes) on Earth. In addition, social media platforms enable people to share information and learn from one another.

Smart devices and wireless networks are almost ubiquitous and are widely available, as is access to online and AI resources. There are, of course, impoverished students who need help from schools to provide them with an internet connection and devices.

What Needs to Happen

Personalization is needed and is possible. What can we do to make personalization happen?

Teachers as Inventors

In *The Teacher as Inventor*, Judith Kleinfeld, Bill McDiarmid, and William Parrett (1986) describe innovative teachers whose work they documented in various small schools. The title captures exactly what I have been calling for to shift the education paradigm. I dream of changes made by teachers. If all teachers are empowered to become inventors—to invent new possibilities with students and enable them to pursue autonomy and personalized learning—we have the chance of accomplishing a paradigm shift.

The authors suggest that teachers should use the small size of a school as an advantage, which is what a school within a school is all about. "Small" makes change easier, especially today, given the widely available resources in technology. The authors recommend that teachers draw on all resources in the school. (When the book was written 40 years ago, technology didn't yet enable access to learning resources from around the world, something we can easily do now.) The authors describe how teachers can draw on resources from the community and broaden students' experiences with travel programs. They also suggest using the technology of the times, such as audio conferencing.

Teachers can become inventors when they are permitted and enabled to do so. I have given some examples of individual teachers who took courageous action to remake students' learning experiences more personalized and more purpose-driven. But most teachers have been taught, and have essentially been forced, to give up their inventive desire. They comply with curriculum standards and are subject to administrative judgment. School leaders need to work on creating space for teachers to become inventive, and policymakers need to look at more than state assessment scores in gauging school performance.

Teachers need to realize that they are creative inventors and that they have the capability and latitude to invent. Whenever I talk to teachers about creating new learning experiences, they always ask me how they would go about doing that. I believe that teachers need to invent their own solutions under supportive conditions. For too long, professional development programs have focused on giving teachers "what they can use next Monday," instead of working with them to help them invent their own solutions. Their solutions are much more likely than some off-the-shelf idea to address the needs and circumstances of their students.

School Leaders as Enablers

Teachers can create the new education paradigm with the support of school leaders. I recently co-authored a book with Jim Watterston, *Focused: Understanding, Negotiating, and Maximizing Your Influence as a School Leader* (2024). Across his 40-year career in education, Watterston has been a school principal, a regional education director, an executive director of large education systems at the state level, and the dean of the faculty of education at the University of Melbourne, Australia. In our book, we argue that leaders should empower and enable others to make decisions about changes. School leaders are not educational philosophers whose job is to get others to implement their philosophy. Rather, their job is to create the conditions for others to generate and implement their own ideas. We also make the case for the need for school leaders to be focused. Instead of trying to do everything, they need to identify and focus on what they can do—and we believe that focus should be working with others to create new possibilities of learning.

Students as Partners

Students can personalize their learning, but educators must create the necessary conditions for this to happen. Students need to be partners in change (Zhao, 2011). I have worked on several projects in more than 30 schools that enable students to personalize their learning and find and solve problems for others. These projects often start with two days of face-to-face meetings with a school team that must include students, teachers, and a school administrator. The first task is often to ask the team to develop their own plan for improving learning. At the end, the teachers and school administrators are always surprised by their students' thinking and abilities, as well as by the students' broad vision of others and their schools. Students can be a great partner in establishing the new paradigm for themselves and for others.

Policymakers as Observers and Supporters

I do not expect education systems to make the paradigm shift overnight. There is too much at stake politically, financially, and regulatorily. Education is one of the most combative public arenas that citizens have a stake in. Any significant change that the public views as detrimental to its expectations and interests can have huge political consequences. Policymakers have to be sensitive to that. Education is also a massive industry that involves the financial interests of a wide variety of people and organizations, such as various businesses; parental, community, and civic groups; and schools of education that prepare teachers and school administrators. Any change that affects the financial interests of such groups can trigger negative reactions and resistance. Education is also highly regulated, with multiple laws and regulations that govern, for example, teacher-student ratios, curriculum and assessment, school governance, teacher accreditation, textbook adoption, standardized tests, school days and hours, and smartphone use. Policy changes would require changes in these areas, which would then require new laws and regulations.

However, I do hope that policymakers would enable all teachers and school leaders to make innovations that contribute to a paradigm shift. The least they can do is not interfere or stop the innovations. If possible, policymakers could offer small grants to inspire and support the changes. In any case, policymakers should collect data about the effects of the innovations and make policies and regulations more flexible.

In Sum

Education needs to change, but the changes must go beyond merely strengthening the traditional paradigm. Most of the changes to date have done little to improve learning for most students or prepare them for a future that is being shaped by rapidly evolving AI technologies (McDiarmid & Zhao, 2022). It's time for a new education paradigm that supports personalization of learning and problem finding and solving.

We need to rely on teachers as the primary inventors who will work with students as partners to create new conditions for learning. We must also rely on school leaders to enable and support teachers to make those changes. Although policymakers are crucial in the beginning of such a transformative shift, they do not need to initiate big changes in policy. Instead, they would best be interested and supportive observers.

The age of AI has arrived. Transformative changes are necessary. They are made by individuals and groups who see the future and want to help prepare our students for that future. I hope you are among them.

References

Anderson, M., Hinz, B., & Matus, H. (2017, November). *The paradigm shifters: Entrepreneurial learning in schools*. Mitchell Institute, Victoria University. https://www.vu.edu.au/sites/default/files/paradigm-shifters-entrepreneurial-learning-in-schools-mitchell-institute.pdf

Apple, M. W., & Beane, J. A. (1995). *Democratic schools*. ASCD.

Armstrong, T. (2012). *Neurodiversity in the classroom: Strength-based strategies to help students with special needs succeed in school and life*. ASCD.

Asia Society. (2008). *Going global: Preparing our students for an interconnected world*. https://asiasociety.org/files/Going%20Global%20Educator%20Guide.pdf

Baker, K. (2007). Are international tests worth anything? *Phi Delta Kappan, 89*(2), 101–104.

Bergeron, P.-J. (2017). How to engage in pseudoscience with real data: A criticism of John Hattie's arguments in *Visible Learning* from the perspective of a statistician. *McGill Journal of Education/Revue des sciences de l'éducation de McGill, 52*(1), 237–246. http://mje.mcgill.ca/article/view/9475

Berliner, D. C., & Biddle, B. J. (1995). *The manufactured crisis: Myths, fraud, and the attack on America's public schools*. Addison-Wesley.

Bonawitz, E., Shafto, P., Gweon, H., Goodman, N. D., Spelke, E., & Schulz, L. (2011). The double-edged sword of pedagogy: Instruction limits spontaneous exploration and discovery. *Cognition, 120*(3), 322–330.

Bruno, C. (2022). The human dimensions: Co-evolution between humans and digital technologies. In C. Bruno (Ed.), *Creativity in the design process: Exploring the influences of the digital evolution* (pp. 15–27). Springer International.

Burnette, J. L., Billingsley, J., Banks, G. C., Knouse, L. E., Hoyt, C. L., Pollack, J. M., & Simon, S. (2023). A systematic review and meta-analysis of growth mindset interventions: For whom, how, and why might such interventions work? *Psychological Bulletin, 149*(3–4), 174–205.

CASEL. (2024, September 17). *More than 8 out of 10 U.S. schools implement SEL, nearly all states have supportive policies*. https://casel.org/more-than-8-out-of-10-u-s-schools-implement-sel-nearly-all-states-have-supportive-policies

CASEL. (n.d.). *Our history*. https://casel.org/about-us/our-history/

Chamberlin, R. (1989). *Free children and democratic schools: A philosophical study of liberty and education*. Falmer.

Cheung, W. M., & Wong, W. Y. (2014). Does lesson study work? A systematic review on the effects of lesson study and learning study on teachers and students. *International Journal for Lesson and Learning Studies, 3*(2), 137–149.

Cipriano, C., Strambler, M. J., Naples, L. H., Ha, C., Kirk, M., Wood, M., Sehgal, K., Zieher, A. K., Eveleigh, A., McCarthy, M., Funaro, M., Ponnock, A., Chow, J. C., & Durlak, J. (2023). The state of evidence for social and emotional learning:

A contemporary meta-analysis of universal school-based SEL interventions. *Child Development, 94*(5), 1181–1204.

Council of Graduate Schools. (2008). *Ph.D. completion and attrition: Analysis of baseline program data from the Ph.D. completion project.* https://cgsnet.org/wp-content/uploads/2022/01/phd_completion_and_attrition_analysis_of_baseline_demographic_data-2.pdf

Council on International Education Exchange. (1988). *Educating for global competence: The report of the advisory council for international educational exchange.* https://eric.ed.gov/?id=ED305833

de Durango, Á. G. (2019, June 9). New York, manure and stairs: When horses were the cities' nightmares. *Smart Water.* https://smartwatermagazine.com/blogs/agueda-garcia-de-durango/new-york-manure-and-stairs-when-horses-were-cities-nightmares

Dean, D., Jr., & Kuhn, D. (2007). Direct instruction vs. discovery: The long view. *Science Education, 91*(3), 384–397.

Dolph, D. (2017). Resistance to change: A speed bump on the road to school improvement? *Journal of Educational Leadership and Policy Studies, 1*(1), 6–20.

Donati, P. (2021). Impact of AI/robotics on human relations: Co-evolution through hybridisation. In J. von Braun, M. S. Archer, G. M. Reichberg, & M. Sánchez Sorondo (Eds.), *Robotics, AI, and humanity: Science, ethics, and policy* (pp. 213–227). Springer International.

Donavel, D. F. (1995). High school: The American walkabout. *Occasional Paper Series, X*(2). Regional Laboratory for Educational Improvement of the Northeast and Islands.

Duckworth, A. (2016). *Grit: The power of passion and perseverance.* Scribner.

Duke, A. (2022). *Quit: The power of knowing when to walk away.* Portfolio.

Durkheim, E. (1893/2014). The division of labor in society. In D. B. Grusky (Ed.), *Social stratification: Class, race, and gender in sociological perspective* (4th ed., pp. 217–222). Routledge. (Original work published 1893)

Durlak, J. A., Weissberg, R. P., Dymnicki, A. B., Taylor, R. D., & Schellinger, K. B. (2011). The impact of enhancing students' social and emotional learning: A meta-analysis of school-based universal interventions. *Child Development, 82*(1), 405–432.

Dweck, C. S. (2000). *Self-theories: Their role in motivation, personality, and development.* Psychology Press.

Dweck, C. S. (2006). *Mindset: The new psychology of success.* Random House.

Eden, M. C. (2019, August 27). The latest education-policy fad amounts to social and emotional engineering. *National Review.* https://www.nationalreview.com/2019/08/new-york-city-schools-curriculum-social-emotional-engineering/

Effrem, K., & Robbins, J. (2019). *Social-emotional learning: K–12 education as new age nanny state.* Pioneer Institute. https://files.eric.ed.gov/fulltext/ED593789.pdf

Ellis, P., Kirby, A., & Osborne, A. (2023). *Neurodiversity and education.* Sage.

Ericsson, A., & Pool, R. (2016). *Peak: Secrets from the new science of expertise.* Houghton Mifflin Harcourt.

Ericsson, K. A. (1996). The acquisition of expert performance: An introduction to some of the issues. In *The road to excellence: The acquisition of expert performance in the arts and sciences, sports, and games* (pp. 1–50). Lawrence Erlbaum.

Every Student Succeeds Act, 20 U.S.C. § 6301 (2015). https://www.congress.gov/bill/114th-congress/senate-bill/1177

Feynman, R. P. (1985). *"Surely you're joking, Mr. Feynman!" Adventures of a curious character.* Norton.

Finn Jr., C. E. (2017, June 19). Why are schools still peddling the self-esteem hoax? Social-emotional learning is rooted in "faux psychology." *Education Week*. https://www.edweek.org/ew/articles/2017/06/21/why-are-schools-still-peddling-the-self-esteem.html

Friedman, H. L. (2022, October 24). The "reality" of kids on television. *Psychology Today*. https://www.psychologytoday.com/us/blog/playing-win/202210/the-reality-kids-television

Friedman, T. L. (2007). *The world is flat: A brief history of the twenty-first century* (Further updated and expanded ed.). Farrar, Straus & Giroux.

Gardner, H. (1983). *Frames of mind: The theory of multiple intelligences*. Basic Books.

Ginsberg, R., & Zhao, Y. (2023). *Duck and cover: Confronting and correcting dubious practices in education*. Teachers College Press.

Gladwell, M. (2008). *Outliers: The story of success*. Little, Brown.

Goldin, C., & Katz, L. F. (2008). *The race between education and technology*. Harvard University Press.

Goldstein, D. (2025, January 29). American children's reading skills reach new lows. *New York Times*. https://www.nytimes.com/2025/01/29/us/reading-skills-naep.html

Gorman, N. (2016, August 8). Critics of social emotional learning standards call it a fad, "non-academic Common Core." *Education World*. https://www.educationworld.com/a_news/critics-social-emotional-learning-standards-call-it-fad-non-academic-common-core-498184814

Greenberg, D., Sadofsky, M., & Lempka, J. (2005). *The pursuit of happiness: The lives of Sudbury Valley alumni*. Sudbury School Press.

Haidt, J. (2024). *The anxious generation: How the great rewiring of childhood is causing an epidemic of mental illness*. Penguin.

Hanushek, E. A., Peterson, P. E., Talpey, L. M., & Woessmann, L. (2019). *The unwavering SES achievement gap: Trends in U.S. student performance*. HKS Faculty Research Working Paper Series RWP19-012. https://www.hks.harvard.edu/publications/unwavering-ses-achievement-gap-trends-us-student-performance

Hanushek, E. A., & Woessmann, L. (2010). *The high cost of low educational performance: The long-run economic impact of improving PISA outcomes*. OECD. https://www.oecd.org/en/publications/2010/01/the-high-cost-of-low-educational-performance_g1ghc4d1.html

Hanushek, E. A., & Woessmann, L. (2012). Do better schools lead to more growth? Cognitive skills, economic outcomes, and causation. *Journal of Economic Growth*, *17*(4), 267–321.

Harris, I. M. (2004). Peace education theory. *Journal of Peace Education*, *1*(1), 5–20.

Hattie, J. (2008). *Visible learning: A synthesis of over 800 meta-analyses relating to achievement*. Routledge.

Hauser, R. M. (2000). *Should we end social promotion? Truth and consequences*. CDE Working Paper No. 99–06. https://cde.wiscweb.wisc.edu/wp-content/uploads/sites/839/2019/01/cde-working-paper-1999-06.pdf

Hess, F. M. (2011). Our achievement-gap mania. *National Affairs, Fall 2011*(9), 113–129. https://www.nationalaffairs.com/publications/detail/our-achievement-gap-mania

Hu, K. (2023, February 2). ChatGPT sets record for fastest-growing user base. *Reuters*. https://www.reuters.com/technology/chatgpt-sets-record-fastest-growing-user-base-analyst-note-2023-02-01/

Hunter, B., White, G. P., & Godbey, G. C. (2006). What does it mean to be globally competent? *Journal of Studies in International Education, 10*(3), 267–285.

Hutton, P. (2022). *Turning around a troubled school: A journey of school renewal*. Future School Alliance.

Jackman, E. D. (1920). The Dalton plan. *The School Review, 28*(9), 688–696.

Johnson, D. W., & Johnson, R. T. (1996). Conflict resolution and peer mediation programs in elementary and secondary schools: A review of the research. *Review of Educational Research, 66*(4), 459–506.

Jones, T. S. (2004). Conflict resolution education: The field, the findings, and the future. *Conflict Resolution Quarterly, 22*(1–2), 233–267.

Kapur, M. (2016). Examining productive failure, productive success, unproductive failure, and unproductive success in learning. *Educational Psychologist, 51*(2), 289–299.

Kapur, M., & Bielaczyc, K. (2012). Designing for productive failure. *Journal of the Learning Sciences, 21*(1), 45–83.

Klahr, D., & Nigam, M. (2004). The equivalence of learning paths in early science instruction: Effects of direct instruction and discovery learning. *Psychological Science, 15*(10), 661–667.

Kleinfeld, J., McDiarmid, G. W., & Parrett, W. (1986). *The teacher as inventor: Making small high schools work*. University of Alaska.

Kuhn, T. S. (1962). *The structure of scientific revolutions*. University of Chicago Press.

Lagemann, E. C. (2000). *An elusive science: The troubling history of education research*. University of Chicago Press.

Lane, D. (2018, January 7). Deschooling in school: Part 1. The Alliance for Self-Directed Education. https://www.self-directed.org/tp/deschooling-in-school/

Lechner, C. M., Bender, J., Brandt, N. D., & Rammstedt, B. (2021). Two forms of social inequality in students' socio-emotional skills: Do the levels of big five personality traits and their associations with academic achievement depend on parental socioeconomic status? *Frontiers in Psychology, 12*: 679438.

Lee, E. A. (2020). *The coevolution: The entwined futures of humans and machines*. MIT Press.

Levin, S., & Engel, S. (2016). *A school of our own: The story of the first student-run high school and a new vision for American education*. New Press.

Lewontin, R. (2001). *The triple helix: Gene, organism, and environment*. Harvard University Press.

Lindsay, J., & Davis, V. (2012). *Flattening classrooms, engaging minds: Move to global collaboration one step at a time*. Pearson.

Liu, J., Peng, P., Zhao, B., & Luo, L. (2022). Socioeconomic status and academic achievement in primary and secondary education: A meta-analytic review. *Educational Psychology Review, 34*(4), 2867–2896.

Loveless, T. (2006). *The 2006 Brown Center report on American education: How well are American students learning?* Brown Center on Education Policy, Brookings Institution. https://www.brookings.edu/articles/the-2006-brown-center-report-on-american-education-how-well-are-american-students-learning/

Macnamara, B. N., & Burgoyne, A. P. (2023). Do growth mindset interventions impact students' academic achievement? A systematic review and meta-analysis with recommendations for best practices. *Psychological Bulletin, 149*(3–4), 133–173.

Mansell, W. (2008, November 21). Research reveals teaching's Holy Grail. *TES*. https://www.tes.com/magazine/archive/research-reveals-teachings-holy-grail

Manzo, K. K. (2008, March 7). Directors of "Reading First" plagued by anxiety over budget cuts. *Education Week.* https://www.edweek.org/teaching-learning/directors-of-reading-first-plagued-by-anxiety-over-budget-cuts/2008/03

Maslow, A. H. (1954). *Motivation and personality.* Harper.

Maslow, A. H. (1999). *Toward a psychology of being* (3rd ed.). Wiley.

McAndrews, T., & Wendell, A. (2002). *Schools within schools.* ERIC Digest.

McDiarmid, G. W., Beghetto, R. A., & Zhao, Y. (2025). *Agents of impact: How education can empower students to change themselves, their communities, and their world.* Solution Tree.

McDiarmid, G. W., & Zhao, Y. (2022). *Learning for uncertainty: Teaching students how to thrive in a rapidly evolving world.* Routledge.

Montessori, M. (1912/2013). *The Montessori method.* Transaction. (Original work published 1912)

Mullis, I. V. S., Martin, M. O., Foy, P., & Arora, A. (2012). *TIMSS 2011 international results in mathematics.* International Association for the Evaluation of Educational Achievement.

Muro, M., Whiton, J., & Maxim, R. (2019, November 20). *What jobs are affected by AI? Better-paid, better-educated workers face the most exposure.* Brookings Institution. https://www.brookings.edu/research/what-jobs-are-affected-by-ai-better-paid-better-educated-workers-face-the-most-exposure/

National Assessment of Educational Progress. (2021). Explore NAEP long-term trends in reading and mathematics. https://www.nationsreportcard.gov/ltt/?age=9

National Center for Education Statistics. (n.d.). Table 3. Number of virtual schools, total state enrollment, total virtual school enrollment, and virtual school enrollment as a percentage of state total enrollment: School year 2019–20. https://nces.ed.gov/ccd/tables/201920_Virtual_Schools_table_3.asp

National Commission on Excellence in Education. (1983). *A nation at risk: The imperative for educational reform.* https://eric.ed.gov/?id=ED226006

National Institute for Direct Instruction. (2014). *Achieving success for every student with direct instruction.* NIFDI Press. https://www.nifdi.org/docman/new-to-di/new-school-handouts/528-achieving-success-for-every-student-with-direct-instruction/file

Neil, A. S. (1960). *Summerhill: A radical approach to child rearing.* Hart Publishing.

OECD. (2018). PISA 2018 global competence. https://www.oecd.org/pisa/innovation/global-competence/

OECD. (2019a). *PISA 2018 results (Volume I): What students know and can do.* OECD Publishing. https://www.oecd-ilibrary.org/education/pisa-2018-results-volume-i_5f07c754-en

OECD. (2019b). *PISA 2018 results (Volume III): What school life means for students' lives.* OECD Publishing. https://www.oecd.org/en/publications/pisa-2018-results-volume-iii_acd78851-en.html

OECD. (2023). *PISA 2022 results (Volume I): The state of learning and equity in education.* OECD Publishing. https://www.oecd-ilibrary.org/education/pisa-2022-results-volume-i_53f23881-en

Page, S. E. (2007). *The difference: How the power of diversity creates better groups, firms, schools, and societies.* Princeton University Press.

Petersen, P. B. (1999). Total quality management and the Deming approach to quality management. *Journal of Management History, 5*(8), 468–488.

Peterson, P. L. (1979). Direct instruction: Effective for what and for whom? *Educational Leadership, 37*(1), 46–48.

Rakesh, D., & Whittle, S. (2021). Socioeconomic status and the developing brain–A systematic review of neuroimaging findings in youth. *Neuroscience & Biobehavioral Reviews, 130,* 379–407.

Reimers, F. (2010). Educating for global competency. In J. E. Cohen & M. B. Malin (Eds.), *International perspective on the goals of universal basic and secondary education* (pp. 183–202). Routledge.

Reimers, F. M. (2008, October 3). Preparing students for the flat world. *Education Week.* https://www.edweek.org/education/opinion-preparing-students-for-the-flat-world/2008/10

Ridley, M. (2003). *Nature via nurture: Genes, experience, and what makes us human.* HarperCollins.

Robbins, J. (2016, August 8). The latest big education fad, social-emotional learning, is as bad as it sounds. *Townhall.* https://townhall.com/columnists/janerobbins/2016/08/08/the-latest-big-education-fad-socialemotional-learning-is-as-bad-as-it-sounds-n2202205

Rose, T. (2016). *The end of average: How we succeed in a world that values sameness.* HarperOne.

Rowe, P. G. (1991). *Design thinking.* MIT Press.

Schwartz, S. (2025, January 29). Reading scores fall to new low on NAEP, fueled by declines for struggling students. *Education Week.* https://www.edweek.org/leadership/reading-scores-fall-to-new-low-on-naep-fueled-by-declines-for-struggling-students/2025/01

Schweinhart, L. J., & Weikart, D. P. (1997). The High/Scope preschool curriculum comparison study through age 23. *Early Childhood Research Quarterly, 12*(2), 117–143.

Schweinhart, L. L., Weikart, D. P., & Larner, M. B. (1986). Consequences of three preschool curriculum models through age 15. *Early Childhood Research Quarterly, 1*(1), 15–45.

Seligman, M. E. P. (2002). *Authentic happiness: Using the new positive psychology to realize your potential for lasting fulfillment.* Atria.

Skinner, B. F. (1954). The science of learning and the art of teaching. *Harvard Educational Review, 24,* 86–97.

Skinner, B. F. (1968). *The technology of teaching.* Prentice Hall.

Skoog-Hoffman, A. Miller, A. A., Plate, R. C., Meyers, D. C., Tucker, A. S., Meyers, G., Diliberti, M. K., Schwartz, H. L., Kuhfeld, M., Jagers, R. J., Steele, L., & Schlund, J. (2024, September 17). Social and emotional learning in U.S. schools: Findings from CASEL's nationwide policy scan and the American teacher panel and American school leader panel surveys. *RAND.* https://www.rand.org/pubs/research_reports/RRA1822-2.html

Smith, A. (1776/2016). *The wealth of nations.* Aegitas. (Original work published 1776)

Solomon, A. (2024, September 30). Has social media fueled a teen-suicide crisis? *The New Yorker.* https://www.newyorker.com/magazine/2024/10/07/social-media-mental-health-suicide-crisis-teens

Spencer, H. (1911). What knowledge is of most worth? In H. Spencer (Ed.), *Essays on education and kindred subjects.* Dent/Aldine. http://www.gutenberg.org/files/16510/16510-h/16510-h.htm

Sternberg, R. J. (1988). *The triarchic mind: A new theory of human intelligence.* Viking.

Stevenson, H. W., & Stigler, J. W. (1992). *The learning gap: Why our schools are failing and what we can learn from Japanese and Chinese education.* Simon & Schuster.

Stillman, J. (2025, January 17). OpenAI CEO Sam Altman says this will be the No. 1 most valuable skill in the age of AI: Nope, it's not IQ, EQ, or adaptability. *Inc.*

https://www.inc.com/jessica-stillman/openai-ceo-sam-altman-says-this-will-be-the-no-1-most-valuable-skill-in-the-age-of-ai/91107542

Suglia, S. F., Saelee, R., Guzmán, I. A., Elsenburg, L. K., Clark, C. J., Link, B. G., & Koenen, K. C. (2022). Child socioeconomic status, childhood adversity and adult socioeconomic status in a nationally representative sample of young adults. *SSM-Population Health, 18*, 101094.

Terhart, E. (2011). Has John Hattie really found the holy grail of research on teaching? An extended review of *Visible Learning*. *Journal of Curriculum Studies, 43*(3), 425–438.

Terrin, É., & Triventi, M. (2023). The effect of school tracking on student achievement and inequality: A meta-analysis. *Review of Educational Research, 93*(2), 236–274.

Tienken, C. H. (2008). Rankings of international achievement test performance and economic strength: Correlation or conjecture? *International Journal of Education Policy & Leadership, 3*(4), 1–15. http://journals.sfu.ca/ijepl/index.php/ijepl/article/view/110/44

Tucker, M. S. (Ed.). (2011). *Surpassing Shanghai: An agenda for American education built on the world's leading systems*. Harvard Education Press.

Tyack, D., & Cuban, L. (1995). *Tinkering toward utopia: A century of public school reform*. Harvard University Press.

University of Wisconsin, Global Competence Task Force. (2008). *Global Competence Task Force report*. http://www.scribd.com/doc/6203902/Global-Competence-Task-Force-Report

U.S. Bureau of Labor Statistics. (2024, August 20). Employment and unemployment among youth—Summer 2024. https://www.bls.gov/news.release/pdf/youth.pdf

Wagner, T., & Dintersmith, T. (2015). *Most likely to succeed: Preparing our kids for the innovation era*. Simon & Schuster.

Washor, E., Frishman, A., & Mejia, E. (2021, January 26). Findings from the Big Picture Learning Longitudinal Study. *Education Reimagined*. https://education-reimagined.org/findings-from-the-big-picture-learning-longitudinal-study

Watters, A. (2023). *Teaching machines: The history of personalized learning*. MIT Press.

Watterston, J., & Zhao, Y. (2024). *Focused: Understanding, negotiating, and maximizing your influence as a school leader*. Corwin.

Wehmeyer, M., & Zhao, Y. (2020). *Teaching students to become self-determined learners*. ASCD.

What Works Clearinghouse. (2020). *What Works Clearinghouse procedures handbook*, Version 4.1. U.S. Department of Education, Institute of Education Sciences, National Center for Education Evaluation and Regional Assistance. https://ies.ed.gov/ncee/wwc/Docs/referenceresources/WWC-Procedures-Handbook-v4-1-508.pdf

Wilson, S. (1958, March 24). It's time to close our carnival. *Life*, pp. 36–37. http://books.google.com/books?id=PlYEAAAAMBAJ&lpg=PA27&dq=alexei%20kutzkov%20life%20magazine&pg=PA25#v=onepage&q&f=false

Zhao, Y. (2009). *Catching up or leading the way: American education in the age of globalization*. ASCD.

Zhao, Y. (2011). Students as change partners: A proposal for educational change in the age of globalization. *Journal of Educational Change, 12*(2), 267–279.

Zhao, Y. (2012). *World class learners: Educating creative and entrepreneurial students*. Corwin.

Zhao, Y. (Ed.). (2016a). *Counting what counts: Reframing education outcomes*. Solution Tree Press.

Zhao, Y. (2016b). From deficiency to strength: Shifting the mindset about education inequality. *Journal of Social Issues, 72*(4), 720–739.

Zhao, Y. (2016c). *The take-action guide to world class learners. Book 1: How to make personalization and student autonomy happen.* Corwin.

Zhao, Y. (2016d). *The take-action guide to world class learners. Book 2: How to "make" product-oriented learning happen.* Corwin.

Zhao, Y. (2016e). Who's afraid of PISA: The fallacy of international assessments of system performance. In A. Harris & M. S. Jones (Eds.), *Leading futures: Global perspectives on educational leadership* (pp. 7–21). Sage.

Zhao, Y. (2017). What works may hurt: Side effects in education. *Journal of Educational Change, 18*(1), 1–19.

Zhao, Y. (2018a). The changing context of teaching and implications for teacher education. *Peabody Journal of Education, 93*(3), 295–308.

Zhao, Y. (2018b). Personalizable education for greatness. *Kappa Delta Pi Record, 54*(3), 109–115.

Zhao, Y. (2018c). *Reach for greatness: Personalizable education for all children.* Corwin.

Zhao, Y. (2018d). Shifting the education paradigm: Why international borrowing is no longer sufficient for improving education in China. *ECNU Review of Education, 1*(1), 76–106.

Zhao, Y. (2018e). *What works may hurt: Side effects in education.* Teachers College Press.

Zhao, Y. (2020a). Another education war? The coming debates over social and emotional learning. *Phi Delta Kappan, 101*(8), 42–48. https://kappanonline.org/another-education-war-social-emotional-learning-debates-zhao/

Zhao, Y. (2020b). Two decades of havoc: A synthesis of criticism against PISA. *Journal of Educational Change, 21*(2), 245–266.

Zhao, Y. (2022a). New context, new teachers, and new teacher education. *Journal of Technology and Teacher Education, 30*(2), 127–133.

Zhao, Y. (2022b). *Learners without borders: New learning pathways for all students.* Corwin.

Zhao, Y. (2022c). Teaching students to identify and solve problems. *Principal Connections, 26*(2), 52–53.

Zhao, Y. (2023). Learning for uncertainty: Reach for greatness. *Educational Research for Policy and Practice, 24,* 129–133.

Zhao, Y. (2024). Artificial intelligence and education: End the grammar of schooling. *ECNU Review of Education, 8*(1).

Zhao, Y. (2025). If schools don't change, the potential of AI won't be realized. *Educational Leadership, 82*(5), 36–40. https://www.ascd.org/el/articles/if-schools-dont-change-the-potential-of-ai-wont-be-realized

Zhao, Y., Basham, J., & Travers, J. (2022). Redefining human talents: Gifted education in the age of smart machines. In R. J. Sternberg, D. Ambrose, & S. Karami (Eds.), *The Palgrave handbook of transformational giftedness for education* (pp. 403–426). Palgrave Macmillan.

Zhao, Y., & Beghetto, R. A. (2024). Effects and side effects: What is missing in education research. *Review of Research in Education, 48*(1), vii–xxviii.

Zhao, Y., Emler, T. E., Snethen, A., & Yin, D. (2019). *An education crisis is a terrible thing to waste: How radical changes can spark student excitement and success.* Teachers College Press.

Zhao, Y., & Zhong, R. (2024). Paradigm shifts in education: An ecological analysis. *ECNU Review of Education, 8*(1).

Zhong, R., & Zhao, Y. (2025). Education paradigm shifts in the age of AI: A spatiotemporal analysis of learning. *ECNU Review of Education, 8*(2).

Index

achievement, visible learning effect on, 11
artificial general intelligence (AGI), 90–91
artificial intelligence (AI)
    to find and solve problems, 64–65
    growth of, 41
    power of, 42, 44–47
    reality of, 91
    to redefine society and the economy, 44–47
    training on, 42–43
    to transform teaching, 43–44
assessment. *See* test scores
audience, developing a sense of, 74
autonomy, student, 53–56, 60

behavior, inquiry-based education vs. direct instruction, 37

change, transformational in education, 80–85
ChatGPT, 41–42
cheating, 43
collaboration, 69–70
confidence, importance of, 33–34
conflict, reasons for, 71–72
COVID-19 pandemic, 24, 46, 73, 91
curriculum, prescribed, 52–56

decision-making, responsible, 27
design thinking, 62
discovery, teaching and, 36–37

East Asian educational systems, 31–35

economy
    growth, predicting with test scores, 34–35
    using AI to redefine, 44–47
education
    changing, 80–85
    in crisis, 1–2
    East Asian vs. Western, 31–35
    establishing a new paradigm of, 88–90
    failure of, 78
    future of, 59
    impact of AI on, 45–47
    inquiry-based vs. direct instruction, 36–38
    modern paradigm of, 89
    policymakers in, 94
    side effects of, 35–36
    Soviet vs. US, 31–33
educational policy and programs, effective for all, 8, 11, 13–14
educational quality, measuring, 33–35
educational research
    effect size, measuring, 8–10
    evidence-based, meaning of, 7–8
    mindset interventions, 16–17
    publication bias, 17
    p-values, 11–13
    randomized samples, 12
    replicability, 12
    risk-benefit measures, 9–10
    social and emotional learning (SEL), 25–27
employment, AI and, 44–45
employment skills, 78–79
entrepreneurship confidence, 34

Every Student Succeeds Act (ESSA), 24
evidence-based, meaning of, 7–8
expertise, developing, 18–19
exploration, teaching and, 36–37

failure, productive, 37–39
fixed mindset, 16

giving up, 15–16, 19–20
global competence
    defined, 72–73
    disappearance of, 67–68
    human interdependence and, 71–74
    importance of, 74–75
    interconnectedness in, 73
grit, 19–20
gritty mindset, 21
growth mindset, 16–17, 19

happiness, requirements for, 29
horse manure, 1–2
human interdependence
    applying the concept of, 70
    basis of, 69–70
    division of labor and, 69
    global competency and, 71–74
    personalized learning and, 68–69
    productive, 71
    tracking and, 69
human talents, AI and the value of, 45, 47

imagination, prisoners of, 81–83
instruction
    differentiated, 13
    effective for all, 8
    effect size, measuring, 8–10
    inquiry-based vs. direct, 36–38
intelligences, 18–19
inventors, teachers as, 92–93

knowledge retention and transfer, 37–39

labor, division of, 69
learning
    impact of AI on, 45–47
    inquiry-based vs. direct, 36–38
    online, 91
    personalized, 29, 51–60, 68–69, 80–81, 90–94
    SEL programs, 25–27
life quality, knowledge acquisition and, 35–37

Masconomet Regional High School, 79
mental health in children, 23
meta-analysis, 10–11
meta-growth mindset, 21
mindsets, 16–17, 19, 21

National Assessment of Educational Progress (NAEP) reading scores, 1
No Child Left Behind (NCLB), 24, 86
No Child Left Behind (NCLB) Reading First program, 7
No Exit (Sartre), 81–83
null hypothesis, 11–13

personal development, elements required for, 27–28
PISA (Programme for International Student Assessment) test results, 1, 31, 33–35, 67, 85
play, teaching and, 35–37
practice, deliberate, 18
problems, finding and solving, 59–65, 74
project-based learning (PBL), 60–63
p-values, 11–13

quitting, 15–16, 19–20

reading achievement, increasing, 7–8
relationships, human-technology, 65
relationship skills, 27

school leaders as enablers, 93
schools
    improving, difficulty of, 77
    innovative, 78–81
    usefulness of, 46–47
    virtual, 46, 91
school within a school (SwS), 83–84, 92
self-actualization, 29

self-awareness, 27
selfish school, 70–71
self-management, 27
self-transcendence, 29
social and emotional learning (SEL), 23–27
social and emotional states in children, 23, 28–29
social awareness, 27
social development, elements required for, 27–28
social intelligence, 70
society, using AI to redefine, 44–47
Soviet Union educational systems, 33
students
    audience, developing a sense of, 74
    autonomy, 53–56, 60
    average, 13
    change, creating, 81
    globally competent, 67
    high-quality, authentic work, 63
    as partners in personalized learning, 93–94
    social and emotional states in, 23, 28–29
success
    inquiry-based education vs. direct instruction, 37
    predicting with test scores, 34

unproductive vs. productive failure, 37–39
suicide rates, 23
sunk cost fallacy, 20

teachers
    as inventors, 92–93
    prisoners of imagination, 82
    process facilitator role, 56
teaching, AI to transform, 43–44
test scores
    declines in, 1–2, 85–86
    East Asia vs. Western, 33–35
    importance of, 34–35
    lack of progress, reasons for, 86–88
TIMSS (Trends in International Mathematics and Science Study), 1, 33–34
tracking, 69

virtual schools, 46
visible learning, 10–11

well-being
    knowledge acquisition and, 35–37
    social and emotional states in children, 23, 28–29
    test scores vs., 35

Study Guide

This ASCD Study Guide is designed to enhance your understanding and application of the ideas and strategies presented in *Fix the Past or Invent the Future: Moving Beyond One-Size-Fits-All Education* by Yong Zhao.

You can use the study guide after you have read the book or as you finish each chapter. The study questions provided are not meant to cover all aspects of the book, but, rather, to address specific ideas that might warrant further reflection.

Most of the questions contained in this study guide are ones you can think about on your own, with a colleague, or in a study group with others who have read (or are reading) *Fix the Past or Invent the Future*.

Chapter 1. Why Probability Research Doesn't Help Classrooms

This chapter critiques the overreliance on "evidence-based" practices, effect sizes, and meta-analyses in education. Zhao argues that statistical averages hide individual differences and can mislead policymakers into implementing one-size-fits-all reforms. Unlike medicine, education often ignores side effects on students who don't fit the "average." Teachers, who know their students best, should use evidence cautiously and embrace personalization rather than panaceas.

1. How have you seen "evidence-based" programs used in your own school or workplace? Did they work equally well for everyone?
2. What risks exist when policymakers apply findings from large studies to all students?
3. Can you think of a time when a program or practice helped some students but harmed others?
4. How might teachers balance scientific evidence with their own professional judgment?

5. If no student is truly "average," what should guide decision making in classrooms?

Chapter 2. Why the Growth Mindset Can Be Stubborn Stupidity

Growth mindset emphasizes perseverance and effort, but Zhao shows its limitations. The research evidence is weak and sometimes biased, and applying the concept blindly can waste time and harm students. Developing talents requires interest, opportunity, and resources, not just persistence. Sometimes quitting is the wiser choice. A *meta-growth mindset* means knowing when to persist and when to walk away, focusing energy on strengths and passions.

1. Have you ever been encouraged to persist at something you disliked or lacked talent for? What happened?
2. When does perseverance become "stubborn stupidity"?
3. How can teachers help students decide when it is best to quit versus when to persist?
4. How does the idea of multiple intelligences challenge the one-size-fits-all use of growth mindset?
5. If you applied a growth mindset only to areas of true interest or strength, how might your learning journey change?

Chapter 3. Why SEL Doesn't Solve Students' Social and Emotional Problems in School

Social and emotional learning (SEL) programs are widespread, but Zhao questions their actual impact. Youth mental health continues to decline despite widespread adoption of SEL curricula. Meta-analyses show only modest effects, and one-size-fits-all approaches ignore individual differences and broader societal issues like social media, politics, and economics. Zhao argues for more meaningful, personalized learning experiences that foster well-being naturally through autonomy, purpose, and relationships.

1. SEL programs are widespread, yet youth mental health continues to worsen. What might explain this paradox?
2. Have you personally experienced or witnessed SEL programs in action? Did they feel helpful, irrelevant, or even harmful?

3. How do larger social issues (politics, technology, economy) affect students' well-being beyond what schools can control?
4. If meaningful learning itself is a better path to social-emotional growth, what would that look like in practice?
5. What role should schools play in addressing mental health, and where should the line be drawn?

Chapter 4. Why Short-Term Wins Can Be Long-Term Losses

Western policymakers often admire East Asian test results, but Zhao warns that focusing on short-term academic wins undermines long-term skills like creativity, curiosity, and adaptability. Although test prep systems may raise scores temporarily, they harm deeper learning and innovation. He highlights the irony that East Asian families often seek Western education for its creativity while Western systems chase East Asian test performance. True success requires valuing long-term growth over short-term metrics.

1. What examples in your own schooling reflect short-term wins (e.g., high test scores) that may have undermined long-term growth?
2. Why do Western countries often envy East Asian test results, while East Asian families admire Western creativity?
3. How can focusing on standardized test preparation harm creativity, curiosity, and transfer of learning?
4. If you were a policymaker, how would you balance short-term accountability with long-term flourishing?
5. How might you redesign learning experiences to prioritize skills and mindsets that matter over a lifetime?

Chapter 5. Why AI Doesn't Help in the Traditional Classroom

AI can be a powerful tool for learning, but only if the educational paradigm changes. In traditional classrooms with prescribed curricula, AI is used to do old tasks slightly better rather than to transform learning. Zhao argues that AI's real potential lies in enabling personalized, student-driven learning where students use AI to explore interests, find problems, and create solutions. Without such a shift, AI risks reinforcing outdated models.

1. In what ways have you or your school used AI so far? Was it mainly to do old things better or to rethink learning?
2. Why does the prescribed curriculum limit the potential of AI in education?
3. Imagine students freely using AI for problem finding and solving. How would their learning look different from today's classrooms?
4. What risks arise if schools adopt AI tools without changing the teaching paradigm?
5. What's one action you could take to use AI in a way that personalizes learning for yourself or your students?

Chapter 6. The Personalization of Learning with AI

Zhao redefines personalized learning as something students do for themselves, not something done to them. True personalization requires freedom from rigid curricula and shifts the teacher's role from instructor to mentor and guide. AI can empower students to design their own pathways, discover passions, and take ownership of learning. The goal is not efficiency but empowerment, unlocking each student's uniqueness.

1. How does Zhao's definition of personalization differ from how schools typically use the term?
2. Think about a time when your learning truly felt personalized. What made it different?
3. What role should students play in personalizing their own learning journeys?
4. What changes would teachers need to make to support student-driven personalization?
5. How might AI tools empower—not replace—student autonomy in learning?

Chapter 7. Problem Finding and Problem Solving

This chapter highlights the importance of cultivating students' ability to discover problems, not just solve them. Traditional education trains students to provide correct answers to known questions, but the future requires creativity, curiosity, and initiative. With AI handling routine solutions, the uniquely human role is to identify new challenges worth addressing. Schools must therefore nurture curiosity and authentic inquiry rather than standardized problem sets.

1. Why is problem finding just as important as problem solving in the age of AI?
2. How often in your education have you been encouraged to ask new questions rather than answer prepackaged ones?
3. Think of a problem in your school, community, or world. How might you reframe it into a project for students?
4. What role can AI play in helping students identify problems worth solving?
5. How can schools encourage curiosity and risk taking instead of sticking to safe, known answers?

Chapter 8. Human Interdependence and Global Competence

Zhao emphasizes that personalized learning should not lead to isolation but to interdependence. By developing unique talents and passions, students can contribute to solving problems for others and the world. This mindset builds global competence—understanding and collaborating across cultural and national boundaries. In a connected world, education must prepare students to use their individuality to enrich the collective good.

1. How do your own talents and interests connect to solving problems for others?
2. What does *global competence* mean to you in your local context?
3. How might schools balance cultivating individual uniqueness with preparing students for global interdependence?
4. Can you think of an example where collaboration across cultures or communities led to innovative solutions?
5. How might AI expand opportunities for students to collaborate globally?

Chapter 9. The School Within a School: A New Approach to Educational Transformation

Systemwide reforms often reinforce the status quo, but Zhao suggests transformation can happen through smaller, bottom-up initiatives. A "school within a school" provides a protected space for innovation, where teachers and students can try new approaches without waiting for systemwide approval. This model empowers local actors to invent change from within, building momentum for larger transformation over time.

1. Why does Zhao argue that top-down reforms often reinforce old paradigms rather than change them?
2. Have you experienced or heard of bottom-up transformations in education? What made them successful?
3. What might a school within a school look like in your setting?
4. What roles should teachers, students, and leaders play in grassroots educational transformation?
5. How could you start experimenting with small-scale innovation inside your current system?

Chapter 10. Where to Go from Here

Zhao calls for teachers to act as inventors, students as partners, and leaders as enablers. Transformation won't be easy, but by shifting mindsets and practices, education can prepare students for an uncertain, AI-driven world. The call is to stop fixing the past and instead invent the future—together.

1. The new paradigm has not coalesced yet, but it will likely include personalization, problem finding and solving, and interdependence. Which element resonates most with you? Why?
2. What challenges might prevent schools from adopting this new paradigm, and how could they be overcome?
3. How can teachers act as inventors, students as partners, and leaders as enablers in your context?
4. Which ideas from the book do you most want to apply in your own life or practice?
5. What concrete next step will you take after finishing this book?

About the Author

 **Yong Zhao**, PhD, is a Foundation Distinguished Professor in the School of Education at the University of Kansas. He previously served as the presidential chair, associate dean, and director of the Institute for Global and Online Education in the College of Education, University of Oregon, where he was also a professor in the Department of Educational Measurement, Policy, and Leadership. Prior to Oregon, Zhao was University Distinguished Professor at the College of Education, Michigan State University, where he also served as the founding director of the Center for Teaching and Technology and executive director of the Confucius Institute, as well as the U.S.-China Center for Research on Educational Excellence. Additionally, he worked as a professor of educational leadership in the Faculty of Education at University of Melbourne and senior researcher at the Mitchell Institute of Victoria University in Australia. He was a visiting Global Professor at University of Bath and a visiting scholar at Warwick University in the UK. He is an elected member of the National Academy of Education and a fellow of the International Academy of Education.

Zhao has received numerous awards, including the Early Career Award from the American Educational Research Association, Outstanding Public Educator from the Horace Mann League of the USA, Distinguished Achievement Award in Professional Development from the Association of Education Publishers, ACEL Nganakarrawa Award, and AECT 2022 Outstanding Digital Learning Artifact Award and Distinguished Development Award. He has been recognized as one of the most influential education scholars. He has published more than 100 articles and nearly 40 books.

Related ASCD Resources

At the time of publication, the following resources were available (ASCD stock numbers in parentheses).

The AI Assist: Strategies for Integrating AI into the Very Human Act of Teaching by Nathan Lang-Raad (#124030)

AI with Intention: Principles and Action Steps for Teachers and School Leaders by Tony Frontier (#124032)

Beyond the Science of Reading: Connecting Literacy Instruction to the Science of Learning by Natalie Wexler (#125006)

The Learning Leader: How to Focus School Improvement for Better Results, 2nd Edition, by Douglas B. Reeves (#118003)

Learning They'll Love: Engage Students, Meet Standards, and Spark Creativity with Personal Interest Projects by Elizabeth Agro Radday (#125019)

Life Skills for All Learners: How to Teach, Assess, and Report Education's New Essentials by Antarina S. F. Amir and Thomas R. Guskey (#121026)

Results Now 2.0: The Untapped Opportunities for Swift, Dramatic Gains in Achievement by Mike Schmoker (#123048)

Students at the Center: Personalized Learning with Habits of Mind by Bena Kallick and Allison Zmuda (#117015)

Teaching Students to Become Self-Determined Learners by Michael Wehmeyer and Yong Zhao (#119020)

Using Technology in a Differentiated Classroom: Strategies and Tools for Designing Engaging, Effective, Efficient & Equitable Learning by Clare R. Kilbane and Natalie B. Milman (#120002)

Well-Being in Schools: Three Forces That Will Uplift Your Students in a Volatile World by Andy Hargreaves and Dennis Shirley (#122025)

For up-to-date information about ASCD resources, go to www.ascd.org. You can search the complete archives of *Educational Leadership* at www.ascd.org/el. To contact us, send an email to member@ascd.org or call 1-800-933-2723 or 703-578-9600.

DON'T MISS A SINGLE ISSUE OF THIS AWARD-WINNING MAGAZINE.

iste+ascd
educational leadership

If you belong to a Professional Learning Community, you may be looking for a way to get your fellow educators' minds around a complex topic. Why not delve into a relevant theme issue of *Educational Leadership*, the journal written by educators for educators?

Subscribe now and browse or purchase back issues of our flagship publication at **www.ascd.org/el**. Discounts on bulk purchases are available.

iste+ascd

Arlington, VA USA
1-800-933-2723

www.ascd.org
www.iste.org